How to be exceptional

read this book

or

be ordinary

how to be exceptional

Written by Stuart Browne

ISBN 978-1-84728-248-4

First Edition

First published October 2006
Published by www.lulu.com

The right of Stuart Browne to be identified as the
Author of this Work has been asserted by him
in accordance with the Copyright, Designs
and Patents Act 1988.

Imagery adapted based on original material from
© iStockphoto.com / Tom Nulens
www.istockphoto.com / www.tomnulens.be

© Stuart Browne 2006

www.zebrasuit.com

How to be exceptional

If you want to be ordinary, don't **read this book**.

How to be exceptional is packed with 45 different ways to think, act and communicate. Each of these models is simple to understand and easy to apply so that you can **start being exceptional immediately**.

If you could take your brain to the gym, this would be its workout; a training circuit that will exercise your awareness, your presence and your attitude so that you **become exceptional at whatever you do**.

About the author

Among his various identities, Stuart Browne is a management consultant, expert communicator, daddy, entrepreneur, creative provocateur, husband, people change specialist, technophile and author.

He's worked as a consultant for PricewaterhouseCoopers, IBM, Xansa and Axon and has advised major organisations including Boots, BP, T-Mobile, Unilever, Unipart, and Xerox. He now runs his own consulting firm.

Through his creative impact, he leaves an indelible trace of inspiration on the people he works with.

His purpose in life is to leave a legacy using his core values of innovation, knowledge and clarity. Part of his legacy will be to help as many people as possible to **become exceptional** at whatever they do.

How to be exceptional offers 45 simple thinking techniques that challenge your mind so that you become what you're capable of instead of just talking about what you could be.

Stuart takes himself just seriously enough to be exceptional in his work and to lead an exceptionally happy, relaxed life with his family, laptop and BMX.

how to be exceptional

Contents

Becoming exceptional 1
Module 1 : Know Yourself 5
    States 6
    The TEA Model 8
    Maps of reality 10
    Values 12
    Who I am 14
Module 2 : Impact 17
    Gravitas bow tie 18
    Contextual Healing 21
    Transmit vs. Receive 24
    Intensity x Frequency 26
    Outcomes and styles 28
Module 3 : Positive mind 31
    Facts vs. Attitudes 32
    Self talk 34
    Tolerations 36
    Reframing 38
    Anchoring 40
    Beware infection 43

how to be exceptional

Module 4 : Strengths First 47
Tribal Archetypes 48
Journey to today 52
Welcome your weaknesses 55
Failure vs. Feedback 57
Dos and Don'ts 59

Module 5 : Influence 63
Rapport 64
Being vague 68
Principles vs. Specifics 71
Unconscious influence 75
Pacing and Leading 76
Talking in Quotes 77
Hot / Cold & Push / Pull 79

Module 6 : Behaviour tuning 87
Bullet time 88
Congruence 90
Head vs. Heart 93
Away vs. Towards 95
Intuiting to action 100
Oblivious + Act 100
Know + Wait 101
Know + Act 101

Module 7 : Awareness of others 105
Motives 106
People are their emotions 110
Sounds, pictures and feelings 115
Filters on reality 118
Perception 121

Module 8 : Attraction 125
    How are you today? 126
    Being interesting 130
    Totems and cults 133
    Submodalities 136
    Rich language 138

Module 9 : Attitude design 143
    Be an expert or authority 144
    Reputation 149
    Recreation 152
    Attitude Designer 154
    Happylogue 161

Trying on a zebra suit 163
Guide to using the models 165
Recommended reading 168

how to be exceptional

Dedicated to all the people who
have made my mind work this way.

You know who you are.

how to be exceptional

Becoming exceptional

Certain people are exceptional. They stand out from the crowd. Whatever they do in their work, lives, hobbies, social circles and communities, they just do it **differently**.

I used the think that I was pretty good at stuff. Then a number of things happened to me that made me realise that there's a huge difference between good and exceptional.

Back then, I worked 60 hours a week, earning a good salary for my efforts. Now, I only do things that interest me and I work no more than 15 days per month. I earn much more than I did back then for less effort and much more enjoyment.

I thought that change was pretty exceptional.

But it wasn't just the outcome of working less and earning more that was exceptional. I was happier and more relaxed. My family enjoyed our time together more and the people I worked with gave me feedback that suggested I was **different**.

I took stock of the things that had happened to me during this period of change and the things that had made the difference in making the difference. I also began to observe other exceptional people and documented the things I noticed.

How to be exceptional is a series of models that, I believe, describe why exceptional people are the way they are.

Some of the material is already in the public domain but has been simplified and re-packaged to make it more understandable. If you're familiar with

how to be exceptional

NLP (Neuro-Linguistic Programming) for example, you may have already used some of the models.

I've distilled some of the best principles from a number of excellent books and websites that I have stumbled upon over time. Some are well known and others less so. I've referenced these within and at the end of the book.

Many of the models are just my opinions of what makes ordinary people exceptional - cool ways to think about stuff that cause you to stop and challenge how you think.

If becoming exceptional is important enough to you, the models will also change what you do.

To define exceptional, you'd think we'd start with a definition of normal. I've taken a different approach and just defined the traits of exceptional people as I see them:

o They have excellent **awareness**; they notice much, much more than most people.

o They have huge personal **presence**; not the way they look necessarily, but how they behave.

o They have a positive and dynamic **attitude**; they think about things differently and are mentally more flexible.

how to be exceptional

How this book works

This isn't just a book, it's a training programme. The programme consists of a series of models. Each model is a thinking technique that's simple to understand and easy to apply.

The models are arranged in 9 modules. Each module requires a few hours of study and has a short exercise at the end so that you can put the models to use. The modules are structured on three levels, each cycling through your **awareness, presence** and **attitude**.

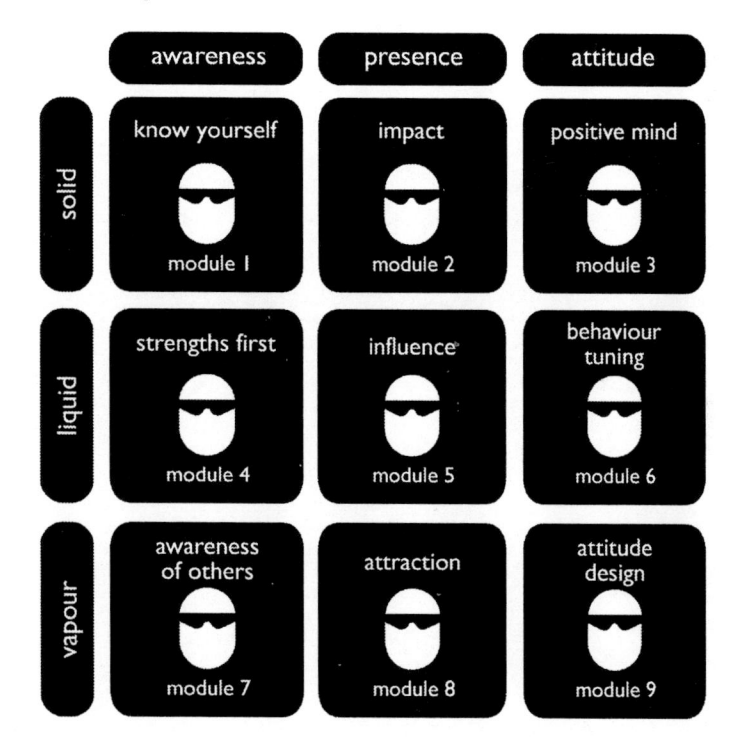

	awareness	presence	attitude
solid	know yourself module 1	impact module 2	positive mind module 3
liquid	strengths first module 4	influence module 5	behaviour tuning module 6
vapour	awareness of others module 7	attraction module 8	attitude design module 9

Some of the concepts in the later modules are more complex and you should take you time moving from one level to the next. Warm things up slowly; treat the ingredients with care as you would when cooking a delicate meal. It will be much easier to digest if you take your time and allow things to infuse properly. The three levels are named **Solid**, **Liquid** and **Vapour**.

how to be exceptional

What do the boxes mean?

Bell boxes like this contain interventions. They are useful statements that prick your mind and set off an **attention alarm**. Most bell boxes ask you to do something in order to make sense of a model.

Pen boxes are mental notes for you to take on each model. If you remember anything, **remember what's in the pen box**. They also serve as quick reminders when you re-read each model.

Homework boxes contain exercises. There are 9 in total; one for each module. The exercises form a crucial part of your understanding and set you off on your path to being truly exceptional.

Who's the cool guy?

Each model has an image featuring a pretty cool character. His purpose is to help you make sense of the models and recall them more easily as you flick through the book again in the future.

Unfortunately, he doesn't have a name.

All I know is that he's **not** Norm.

He's far from Norm.

awareness
know yourself

Module 1 : Know Yourself

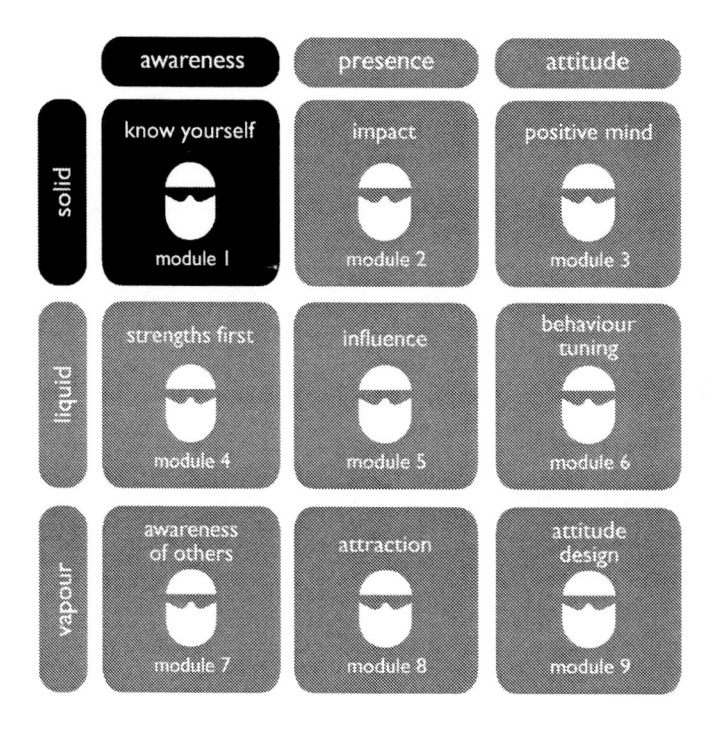

	awareness	presence	attitude
solid	know yourself module 1	impact module 2	positive mind module 3
liquid	strengths first module 4	influence module 5	behaviour tuning module 6
vapour	awareness of others module 7	attraction module 8	attitude design module 9

If you don't know yourself, what do you know? Self awareness is the explicit understanding that you exist.

People who are self conscious worry about how they may appear to others.

Self awareness is different; it's about being acutely aware of yourself and noticing the unconscious things that you do so that you can control and adjust them.

During this module, you will begin to get to know yourself more intimately.

how to be exceptional

States

You are in a state of mind constantly. Whatever you say and do is done though a particular state of mind.

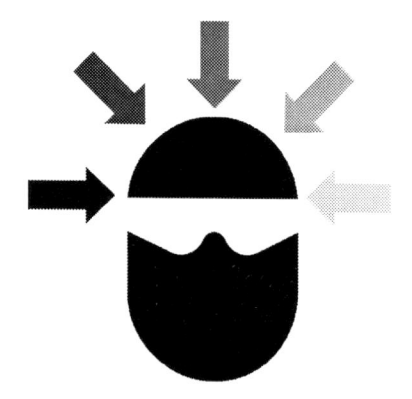

Your state of mind affects how you think. It affects the words you use. It affects how you respond to what others say.

Hypnotists use the term **altered state** to describe what they call a trance. They know that the state of mind that you are in is crucial to the way that you act on their suggestions. So, the first thing they do is work on noticing and changing your state.

If a hypnotist can change somebody's state to get a certain result, I'd suggest that you can probably notice and change your own state with minimal effort.

Think back to a time when you have said things that you later wished you hadn't. What was your state immediately before you spoke?

It's likely that you can remember what you said much more readily than you can remember your state.

That's because our states are mostly unconscious.

Negative states of mind drag you down. There is little point trying to do something exceptional if you're in a negative state.

awareness
know yourself

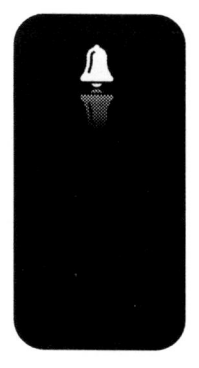

> Now, if you haven't already started, begin to notice the state you're in now. Once you decide what it is, start to imagine what it would be like to be even more in that state.
>
> If you're relaxed, imagine what it would be like to relax more. If you're focused, imagine what you would do if you were even more focused.

Becoming aware of your state is the first step in becoming exceptional. If you can match your state of mind to what you want to achieve, you will perform to a higher standard.

Once you notice the state you're in, you have a choice.

> "The highest possible stage in moral culture is when we recognize that we ought to control our thoughts."
>
> **Charles Darwin**

You can either avoid doing things that don't match your state – like not painting your front door if you're in a state of frustration.

Or, you can choose to control and then change your state to one that's more suitable to whatever it is that you want to do.

> Become aware that you always have a state of mind.
>
> Getting into the right state is like an actor getting into costume.
>
> Before you perform, check your costume and only perform when you know it's appropriate for the performance you're about to deliver.

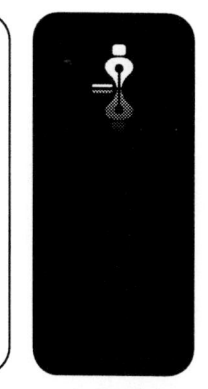

The TEA Model

Now that you're more aware of your **state**, I want to introduce a technique that you can use to control and manage it. The premise of the TEA Model is that your **T**houghts drive your **E**motions and your **E**motions drive your **A**ctions – hence the **TEA** acronym.

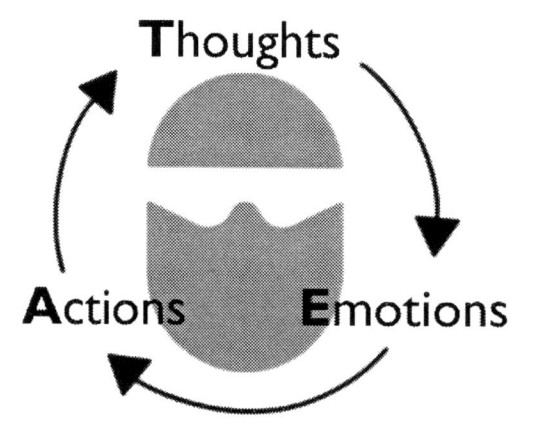

Thoughts

Actions   **Emotions**

In turn, your **A**ctions drive your **T**houghts. It's becomes a self fulfilling cycle.

Noticing your emotional **state** allows you to use your **thoughts**, such as the images and words that you create in your mind, and your **actions**, such as your posture, language and facial expressions to break the cycle.

It sounds extraordinary that you change your **state** by thinking differently or by doing different things. But how do you think you get into negative emotional **states** in the first place? It's usually by doing (actions) or thinking (thoughts) negative things.

> Take a moment to relax completely. Slouch down lower in your chair and let your arm drop to your side. As you relax more, allow your head to roll right back.
>
> Now, breathe in deeply through your nose and slowly let out the biggest sigh you possibly can. As you exhale, try to feel as motivated and focused as you can.

awareness
know yourself

It makes sense then, that doing the opposite can change your state for the better. Positive actions and thoughts lead to positive emotions.

> Now sit upright with the base of your spine right in the corner of your chair. Roll your shoulders backwards so that your back is straight and tilt your head back slightly. Think of the best you've ever been at something.
>
> **Now** feel as motivated and focused as you can.

In module 3, we'll look at **anchoring** and find out how you can attach certain **states** to everyday things that you see and do. For now, all I want you to be aware of is that you have a **state** and that there's a method that can be used to change it.

Thinking about great things puts you into a **great state**. Thinking about happy things puts you into a **happy state**. Talking in a serious tone puts you into a more **serious state**. Sitting in a relaxed position puts you into a **relaxed state**.

It really is that simple.

> The **TEA** metaphor is a useful one; from now on, whenever you **notice your state**, I want you to decide whether it's time to **take a TEA break** and do something about it.
>
> As you begin to do this, you'll start to notice how easy it is to **identify your state and adjust it**.

how to be exceptional

Maps of reality

Whether you like it or not, whatever you think is **right** or **real** or **true** isn't. You're only ever considering your own personal map of reality and not reality itself.

Because we've all had a unique set of personal experiences, with no two people being identical in their lives, we all have different personal **maps of reality** and therefore differing opinions.

Although there are certain things that you can be sure of, most things are just your opinion based on the experiences that you've had in your life so far.

Becoming aware that you **only** have a **map of reality** helps you do something really useful on your journey to becoming exceptional.

When you make statements to other people, you can begin to use some powerful prefixes:

- In my view…
- I think that…
- Would anybody disagree…?
- In my World…
- From where I'm standing…
- I get the feeling that…

These pre-fixes to your statements enable you to couch opinions in a way that allows others to understand that it's **only your** thinking and that you're open to the **fact** that **they** may have different opinions.

awareness
know yourself

Because people notice that you notice them more, this is an incredible **rapport** building technique and, as part of the deal, you will also become more aware that there are many different opinions out there.

Once you notice this, you will start to explore why peoples' opinions are different. From there, you will gain much greater insight, information and knowledge that would usually bypass your **awareness**.

> Take a few moments and consider something you've said recently that was based on your unique experience and which might not be 'true' in somebody else's map of reality.
>
> o It may be an opinion you've expressed as a fact.
>
> o It could be a view you have based on something you've seen or heard before.
>
> Now, notice how you could have framed that statement so that it was clear to others that it was based on your own map of reality.

If you don't do this then the people who you interact with every day probably have opinions of you that aren't as useful to you as they could be.

> Realise that nobody is right; including you. Everything that you say is based on the way that you experience things. So, if something is only your **map of reality**, say so. Make it clear to others that it is your opinion.
>
> Everything is some form of hallucination and everybody is hallucinating.

Values

In my humble opinion, you can't decide what your values are; you can't sit in a room with a pen and paper and brainstorm what you'd like your values to be and then suddenly start living by them.

You are **given** your values based on your unique experience of the World.

Parents and close family, teachers, friends, the government and the media all supply us with information that we absorb and digest in order to form our own personal values.

Values are something you get, not something you choose and although you can change them over time, they form a deep rooted part of who you are and why you do things.

You're also responsible for giving the people around you their values in exactly the same way – whether you mean to or not.

Many people find it hard to establish what is or isn't a value. So I'm going to give you my view and explain why I think it's important that you clearly establish your values.

In my experience, values are **principles** in your life which recur and drive common behaviour. They are the things that you are **emotionally attached to at an unconscious level**.

Example values are things like: Change, Accuracy, Tidiness, Creativity, Honesty, Knowledge, Trust, Independence, Family, Progress, Pleasure, Status, Discipline and Variety.

awareness
know yourself

> Throughout this programme, you'll notice the terms **conscious** and **unconscious**. You won't hear the word subconscious from me.
>
> That's because one of my personal values is that that the unconscious is more powerful than the conscious.
>
> The prefix of 'sub' - meaning 'under' - infers that it's less powerful than the conscious. It takes belief in the unconscious to be exceptional.

The reason that your values are so important is precisely because of the emotional attachment that you have with them; because they are a deep part of who you are, they are hard to change. If something is important enough to unconsciously drive your behaviour, I believe that you should take time to understand **specifically** what it is.

So, **clarify your values**. Take time out to list the things that you are emotional bound to. Assess whether they repeatedly drive your behaviour and, over a period of time, refine what you believe to be your key values.

Once you clarify your values, you can begin to live by them **consciously**. You can tell others what your values are so that they are able to make more sense of why certain actions and decisions are important to you.

> Clarify the things that are unconsciously driving your behaviour. Once you clarify them, you can begin to **consciously** live your life by them.
>
> Values run through your veins.
>
> They should also be worn on your sleeve.

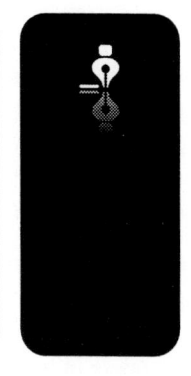

Who I am

If you're really **aware** of yourself, you must be able to state who you are. When you're comfortable with the way that you describe yourself to yourself, you start doing more of the things that you enjoy and focus on what you do well.

For generations, people have searched for the meaning of life. Some theorise and speculate, many just give up; the question proving too difficult to comprehend. Although you can never be sure if you've answered the question 'what's the meaning of life?' in a general sense, you can at least begin to answer it for yourself.

> I'm a teacher
> I'm a mother
> I'm a husband
> I'm an accountant
> I'm an artist
> I'm a healer
> I work in a bank
> I'm kind
> I fix cars
> I live to enjoy life
> I'm incomplete

Your **values** provide a big part of the answer, but they only describe you at a certain level and there are many ways that people can use to describe themselves.

Take time out and state who you believe you are. After all, you live every day of your life as you. Your **values** and **who I am** statement are crucial to this programme and you will build on them in each module.

There's little point walking around being somebody if you don't know who it is. When you ask yourself who you are, you **become introspective** and look for meaning. Start to **be more self aware**.

Write down your 'who I am statement'. If there are many different versions of you, write them all down.

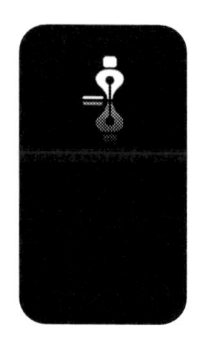

awareness
know yourself

Module 1 - Exercise

Take some time out before the next module and begin to **clarify** your **values**.

As you do this, just as you used to practise your signature when you first learned 'real writing', begin to practise your **who I am** statement.

By the time you've finished, you should have one list of values and a second statement (or list) describing who you think that you are.

how to be exceptional

presence
impact

Module 2 : Impact

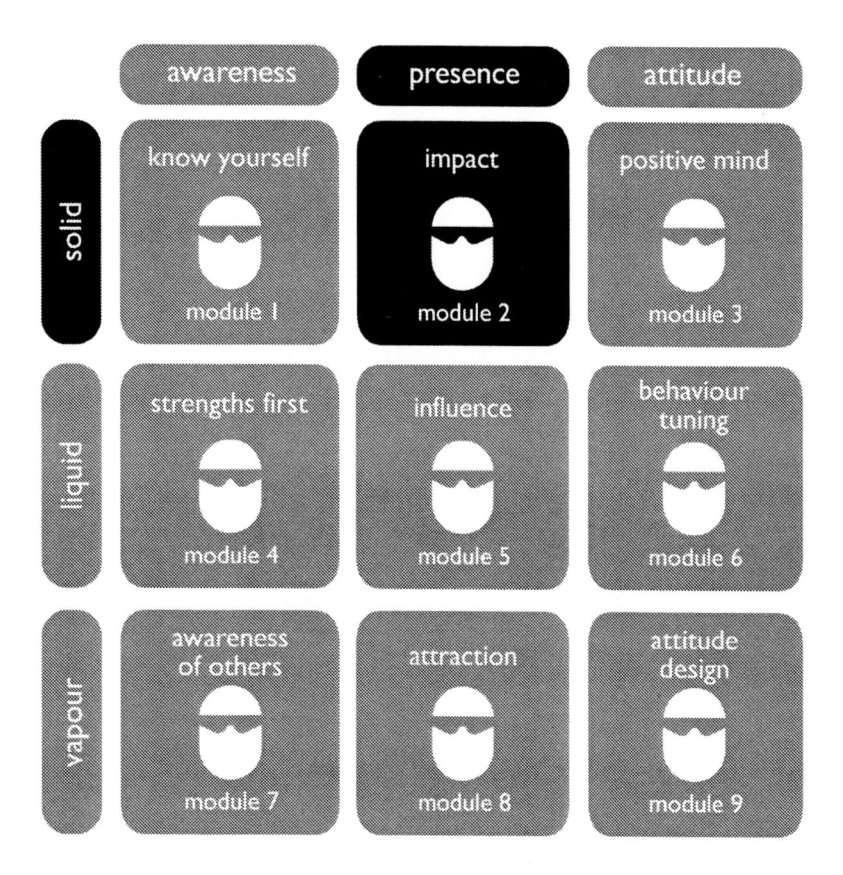

	awareness	presence	attitude
solid	know yourself	**impact**	positive mind
	module 1	module 2	module 3
liquid	strengths first	influence	behaviour tuning
	module 4	module 5	module 6
vapour	awareness of others	attraction	attitude design
	module 7	module 8	module 9

The height of presence is impact. The more able you are to make an impact on others, the more presence you will have.

How you communicate and behave are crucial to your impact. Module 2 introduces a range of models that you can use as cornerstones of your personal impact.

how to be exceptional

Gravitas bow tie

Have you noticed how certain people have gravitas and others don't? You may have wondered why the ones that have it have it. What's so different about these people that gives them such impact?

I'm going to suggest that everybody has gravitas; it is just present in different quantities for each person. Gravitas isn't a **yes** or **no** thing. It's like weight; you have a certain level of it naturally and you can do things that increase it or reduce it.

My interest in gravitas started the first time I heard somebody describe a colleague as having it. I wondered what gave that person gravitas and whether they knew **that**, and **why** they had it.

I studied nearly everybody that I worked with to establish what gave them the level of gravitas that they had and the things that undermined their gravitas in certain situations.

The **gravitas bow tie** has been designed to make it easier for you to build and maintain gravitas in the situations that you find yourself in. It focuses on two key ingredients of gravitas; your **style** and your **knowledge**.

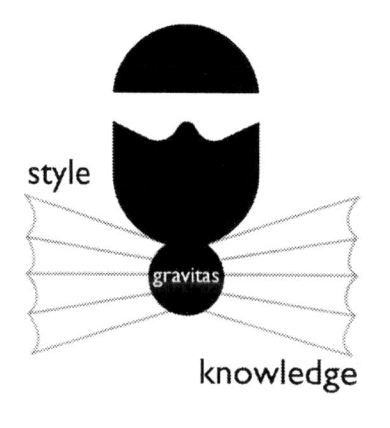

- People who have gravitas have a **definitive and natural personal style**. They use it deliberately, confidently and consistently.

- People with gravitas also speak with **great knowledge** on the subjects that they discuss. They stick to the things they know best.

presence
impact

If you want more gravitas, design a definitive personal style that you are comfortable with. A look, a way of holding yourself, mannerisms, trademark phrases and words, a voice tone, a pace of speaking, how you engage people's eyes.

Work on it and use it very deliberately. Become more aware of the traits you have that might cause other people not to take notice of you and the tiny things you do that are inconsistent. Then adjust them.

> A person with gravitas once gave me and the team that I was working with the best meeting preparation I've ever had. He said "When somebody in the team makes a point, before you add to it, stop yourself and ask 'is what I'm about to say going to at least double the impact of their statement?'
>
> If the answer is 'no' then say nothing"

Sticking to the things that you know best gives you a natural confidence. Whether this is talking about what you already know most about or conducting thorough research and preparation before you speak to people, you'll find that your gravitas will increase when you don't stray from the beaten path. It is also easier to be passionate about things that you understand best.

Your knowledge may be an area of **expertise**, a **skill** or even a **position** on a football field. Knowledge isn't just about speaking, it's about doing. You need to have deep knowledge, possibly at an unconscious level, to be able to perform any role exceptionally well.

If you consider the gravitas bow tie when you watch people interact, you'll notice that there are people with style and weak knowledge and there are people with knowledge and poor style. You'll soon notice what it is they're doing that limits their gravitas. Watch them and learn. Then work on your own style and knowledge domains.

how to be exceptional

Make your own gravitas bow tie; start with a central circle and draw lines on either side to form two triangular sections of a bow. The five lines on the left should lead to individual statements that define your **natural style**. On the right, the five lines should lead to five statements that describe your **knowledge**; the things you know and do best.

When you've completed your bow tie you can imagine putting it on whenever you want to have more gravitas. Wear it with pride and your impact will increase immeasurably.

When you want to have gravitas, operate a **definitive** and natural **style**. Be aware of the way that you appear to others and then choose a way of holding yourself, a series of traits and a way of performing that add up to a personal style that you are most comfortable with.

If you try to be somebody you're not — it will be obvious and will ultimately undermine your gravitas.

When you want more gravitas, stick to what you're best at.

Every time you '**erm…**' you show a lack of knowledge.

If you stick to what you know best, you will be confident and your gravitas will increase.

If you research, practice and prepare the things you don't know so well, your gravitas will increase.

If you stay silent or take a back seat when others are doing what they do best, your gravitas will increase.

presence
impact

Contextual Healing

When we communicate, we either do it consciously or unconsciously. Sometimes we are considered about the things we say and at other times we say the first thing that occurs to us. Good communicators not only consciously decide **what** to say, but they consciously decide **how** to deliver it.

> Have you ever asked somebody to do something and been astounded at how different what they did was from your expectation?
>
> Usually, **if somebody doesn't do what you asked for, you did a bad job of asking for it**.

So much communication is misinterpreted because the person delivering it has designed its delivery ineffectively. There are many factors involved in structuring good communication but by far the simplest and most effective technique that I have encountered is **Contextual Healing** - a model that makes you consider the content of your message and bandage it in the appropriate contextual terms.

It's based on the notion that all really good messages have a structure to them:

They have a certain **context** that makes the message meaningful and a **process** that describes how the message fits in the broader scheme of things.

Finally, they have **content**.

Good communication structure:

- Context is about **why**
- Process is about **how**
- Content is about what, where and with whom

Most poor communicators only give content. Without the context and process, the recipients of their messages do the logical thing; they make up their own context and process. Little wonder there are such differences between what you ask for and what you get.

This model can be used with both verbal and written communication. It is a really effective way of structuring e-mails – most of my e-mails are now three paragraphs, one for each element of this model.

It's also a great way to structure reports, speeches and presentations; the best reports always have a 'purpose' section that outlines why the author has decided to write the report. The purpose section (context) will put the reader or audience in a **state** that will affect how they absorb the rest of the content.

Consider these examples with and without context and process:

With	Without
I have to go and spend an hour on the phone.	I've decided to improve my personal performance so that I can be more effective at work and spend more time at home. The course I'm doing uses tele-classes and starts at 7 o'clock. So, **I have to go and spend and hour on the phone.**

presence
impact

With	Without
Could you produce a sales report for me?	We're 20% behind our sales target. There is a sales meeting tomorrow to discuss actions to pull each department back in line. **Could you produce a sales report for me?**
Put your shoes on.	Your sister's just dropped a glass in the kitchen. Mum's gone to get the dustpan. **Put your shoes on.**

When you deliver any communication, it will make a greater impact and get a better response if you consider the context and process in addition to the content.

Context and process give content more meaning.

Transmit vs. Receive

Communication technology has advanced phenomenally in the past 20 years. But the unprecedented mediums haven't been the Buck Rogers style video watches predicted by futurologists two decades ago.

The most popular forms of communication have been asynchronous ones - where the recipient and sender of information do not converse in real time. SMS text messages and e-mails are both examples of this style of communication along with Citizen Band (CB) radio three decades ago.

These technologies haven't existed instead of real time communication mechanisms but have grown up along side them.

Their popularity is down to the fact that they adhere to a base principal of communication; it consists of transmission and receipt of information. When we do one, we stop doing the other. When you communicate, you either **transmit** or **receive.**

There's a cliché that says 'you have two ears and one mouth for a reason.' The inference that most people take from this is that we should listen twice as much as we speak. But every time two people held a three minute conversation there would be a minute of silence – hardly efficient.

> Have you ever been so busy waiting to make a point that by the time it's your turn to speak, you have forgotten what you were going to say? Or, perhaps somebody else made the point and you failed to realise they'd said it because you were too focused on finding your own transmission spot?

presence
impact

People have a natural and comfortable level of **transmit and receive**.

Some people are high transmitters and spend most of their time talking. Others are strong receivers and spending more time listening.

During any interaction, you can plot where people lie in terms of their contribution to the communication.

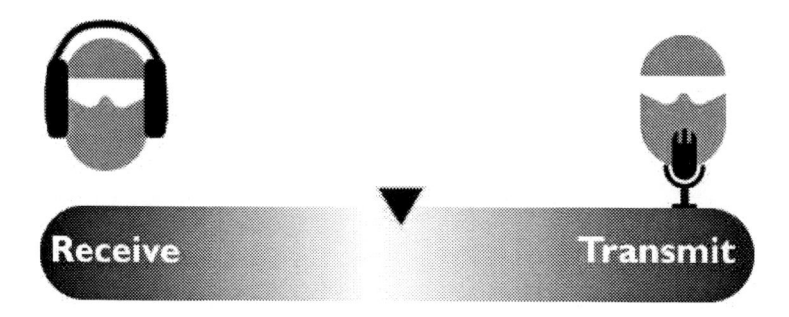

Receive ▼ Transmit

I don't believe that there's a right place to be on this communication continuum but there are definitely wrong places to be if you want to make an impact. **Avoid the extremities and find a balance point**.

o   If you never transmit, you'll have weak presence.

o   If you never shut up, you'll undermine your presence.

> Begin noticing where you are on this continuum.
>
> During and after conversations, plot your balance point. Avoid either end and you'll create a bigger positive impact.

Intensity x Frequency

Study wave theory and you'll find that the power of a wave of sound or light is proportional to its intensity and frequency. An intense high frequency wave is more potent than a low frequency less intense wave.

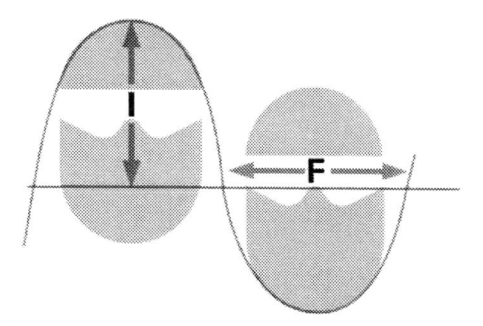

The same is true for communication. The power of your messages is based on how often you deliver them and how intensely you deliver them.

If you want to make an impact with your communication, use intensity or frequency, or both.

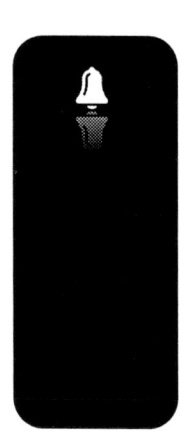

Impact = Intensity x Frequency

> Have you ever encountered people who deliver the same message every day with resounding monotony?
>
> How much notice do you take of them?
>
> Contrast this with listening to an impassioned speech at an annual conference. You're likely to remember this at the following annual conference and probably the next two or three.

When you deliver a message, connect with your recipients at an **emotional** level. Decide not just what you want them to **hear**, but how you want them to **feel** during and after they hear it.

presence
impact

Choose your mediums of delivery so that the message is repeated sufficiently to be recalled by your recipients. The nature of this obviously depends on the message and recipients but generally, the frequency should be appropriate to the significance of the message. Too infrequent and people won't recall it and act on it. Too often and you'll sound like a stuck record and people will switch off.

Tips for intensity

- Once you have chosen the correct emotional **state** for your recipients, choose words that strike that emotional chord.

- Make your voice tone and language **congruent** with your message using the models covered in module 5.

- Use the **submodalities** that are covered in detail in module 8.

Tips for Frequency

- If you're getting bored of saying something, everybody else is probably already there.

- Vary your medium over time.
    - in person and over e-mail
    - **words** and **pictures**

- Consider getting other people to deliver your message in addition to you, varying the messenger over time.

how to be exceptional

Outcomes and styles

Outcomes are really important; they are the things that you get for your efforts. However, some people focus on reaching **outcomes** without considering the **style** in which they achieve them.

Deliver that project; hit your sales target; score that goal; arrive for the meeting on time; write that report; deliver that presentation.

People can achieve exactly the same outcome in completely different ways. Goals in football are worth the same whether they are miscued and speculative or involve lobbing the goalkeeper from the half way line.

What marks out truly exceptional people is the **style** with which they reach their **outcomes**. Good people just reach outcomes; **exceptional people reach outcomes with style**.

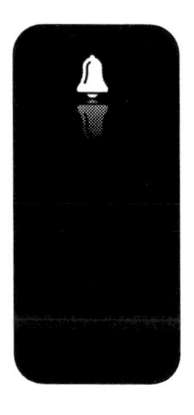

> Have you ever been to Rome? If you haven't, you should. It's one of the most amazing cities in the World. You really get a sense for what it would have been like thousands of years ago. Standing in the Coliseum you can almost feel the roar of the crowd and hear clanking swords as you stand looking at the now eroded stonework and mighty arches. Then there's the local food and amazing Italian wine – it really is a wonderful place to relax....

Your outcomes are the **destination** and your style is the **journey**. The journey itself can be as significant as the destination.

presence
impact

> Imagine travelling to Rome from London. You board the Orient Express and take your time crossing Europe, stopping off in Venice to stretch your legs; dining in 5 star luxury with nothing to distract you from the splendour but the gentle rocking of the carriage and the spectacular changing scenery of each country you speed through.
>
> Each evening, you wear the clothes that make you feel extra special. You eat the finest food and take your time to enjoy the company that you're in and the conversations that you have.

Style is not only part of your personal **gravitas**; it is also a crucial part of your **identity**. Style is what sets apart exceptional people from everybody else. It's the most noticeable aspect of your presence at an **unconscious** level and gives you away when everything else you do is perfect.

- Deliver a perfect presentation with a coffee stain on your tie and they'll remember the perfect presentation last.
- Argue with the referee and get booked for dissent; spectators will remember that skill along with all of you others.
- Use MS Comic as your e-mail font; it's called 'comic' for a reason.
- Walk in to an interview and trip over the doorstop and your killer CV won't be as credible as it was.
- Enter into office gossip; it won't be long before you're the subject of it.

> The one thing that I want you to remember about your **presence** is that the **style** with which you do things is at least as important as the outcomes you get.
>
> Sometimes style is even more important.

Module 2 - Exercise

- List the 5 key attributes of your **style** that will give you more gravitas.

- List the 5 key **knowledge** areas that you can discuss or do with gravitas.

Once you have this, ask 3 people what words they would use to describe your style. Then ask 3 people which subjects they think you know the most about or what you do best.

Oh, and give them some context and explain the process you're going through!

attitude
positive mind

Module 3 : Positive mind

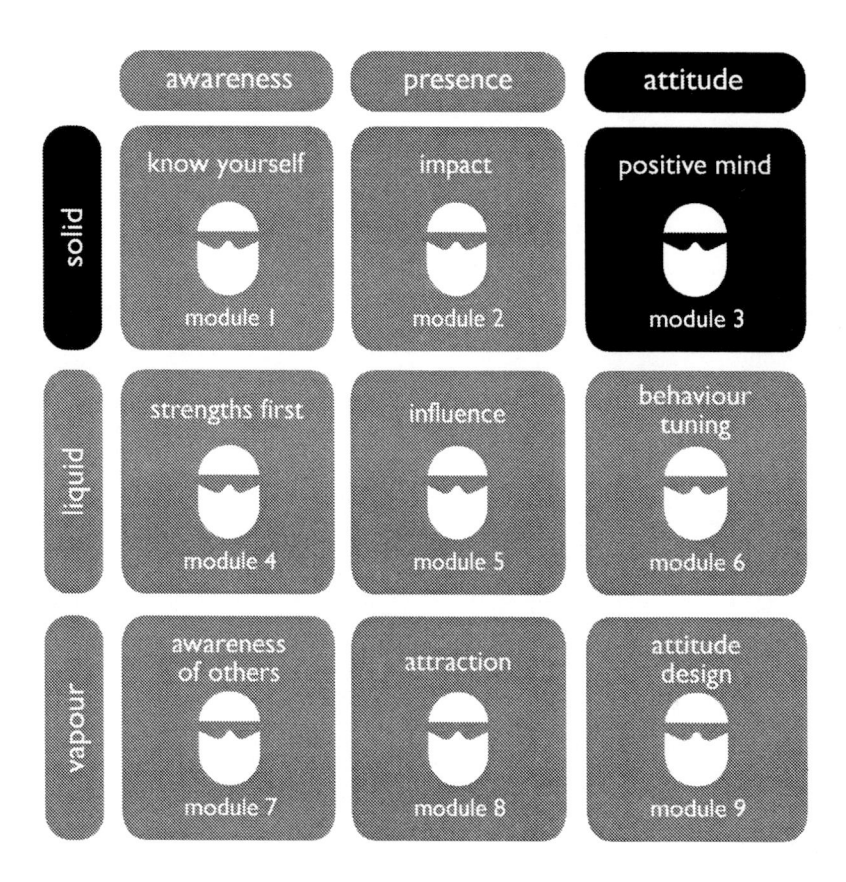

	awareness	presence	attitude
solid	know yourself — module 1	impact — module 2	**positive mind — module 3**
liquid	strengths first — module 4	influence — module 5	behaviour tuning — module 6
vapour	awareness of others — module 7	attraction — module 8	attitude design — module 9

A positive mental attitude is the most powerful resource available to you because positive people achieve heroic things.

Module 3 shows you how to build, maintain and amplify your positivity.

Facts vs. Attitudes

There are **facts** and there are **attitudes** to facts. Most of the time, people can't change facts. But anybody can change their attitude to a fact if they want to.

Your attitude is a choice; you get to **decide how you feel** about something - nobody can decide for you.

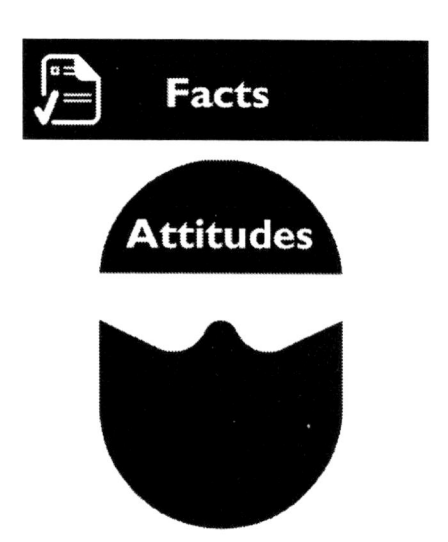

Although people can behave in certain ways that change your attitude, ultimately it is you who decides to change your attitude based on the facts that people present you with.

As soon as you realise that **attitude is a choice**, you become more exceptional. You become more exceptional because minor obstacles don't affect your focus. You find other ways of dealing with what those around you tag as **stress**.

Facts are obstacles and your attitude is a way of overcoming that them.

I used to work full-time for a consulting firm. The nature of the work meant that I was away from my family for five days each week. It would have been easy to accept the fact that my employer wanted me to work away from home and adopt a 'that's life' attitude.

Instead, I changed my attitude to 'I need to create a way of earning the same in half the time'. The new attitude helped me deal with the fact that I was away from home and, at the same time, transformed my lifestyle and income.

attitude
positive mind

> Remember the last time you were in a car and somebody did something that put you in danger.
>
> Maybe they cut you up at a roundabout or pulled out in front of you on the motorway. Do you remember how you felt during and just after the event?
>
> Whatever they did was a **fact**. However you responded was your **attitude** to that fact. Many people automatically and unconsciously decide to adopt an attitude that isn't immediately useful to them. Getting road rage for example isn't going to change the fact that the other driver did what they did.

When people are stressed, if the source of their stress is a fact, they will continue to be stressed until they adopt a different attitude to the fact.

If you just accept facts, you become negative. If you decide to see facts as obstacles that you can easily overcome, you immediately become positive.

I also strongly believe that eliciting your attitudes to facts makes you more creative. When you switch your negative attitude to a negative fact to a positive attitude, you immediately become more able to generate innovative ways of challenging the fact.

> The key to maintaining a positive mind is noticing the difference between a fact and your attitude to the fact.
>
> Once you have the **fact** and your **attitude** to it in **separate boxes**, you can begin to change.
>
> Tune yourself into the facts that are stopping you being completely positive and change your attitude to them.

how to be exceptional

Self talk

Allow me to let you into a **secret** that may shock you. Do you know that **voice** you get in your head from time to time? We'll, it isn't just you who has it; everybody has one. Some people actually have a few of them chattering away in there.

Internal dialogue is important. Without it, we wouldn't have an opportunity to practise what we want to say before we say it. We wouldn't be able to think things through and consider the options, challenges, alternatives and benefits.

The problem is this - **the little character in your head doesn't know when to shut up**. It probably talks to you when you're walking down the street, having important conversations and exercising.

Sometimes it will say good things that make you feel great, other times it will say negative stuff that brings you down.

Think of a situation where you get nervous or uneasy.

Go back to a memorable time when this happened and notice what your internal voice was saying to you.

Notice where in your head it was coming from (yep – it moves around in there too) and notice the voice tone it was using.

attitude
positive mind

Here's the **really big secret**:

It is actually **your** voice.

You are creating it, so **you** can change it.

> Now, imagine yourself in the same situation in the future. Just before the little character starts to speak:
>
> o Move it to a different place. It can even go outside of your head if you want it to
>
> o Change its voice to Mickey Mouse or Elma Fudd
>
> o Slow it down to half speed
>
> o Make it end whatever it says with the words '…I am SO cool'

Your **Thoughts** in the **TEA model** are **self talk.** Noticing your self talk voice and ensuring that it's useful to you is a big factor in being exceptional.

If you have a negative self talk voice nagging away at you while you're trying to perform at your best, take action.

> That voice in your head is self talk and it's there all of the time. Notice it and make sure it's useful to what you're doing or about to do. If it's not useful, change it.
>
> It's your voice and **you are in control** of it.

how to be exceptional

Tolerations

The things we tolerate are those that are important enough to cause us a niggling pain but not important enough for us to do something about.

Tolerating is like having a stone in your shoe that moves around and causes you to hobble occasionally before going away again.

You can't be exceptional with stones in your shoes. Most of the time, the stuff you tolerate isn't hard to fix. Nor is it causing you great pain. That's why you tolerate it.

View your tolerations as low hanging fruit that you can pick **immediately** to **become more exceptional**.

> "Tolerance is another word for indifference."
>
> **Somerset Maugham**

When you list your tolerations, you can begin to work on them.

So, list yours and sort them quickly.

If they can't be sorted quickly, discuss them with the people around you who either cause them or share their impact. That way, you'll stand a better chance of fixing them.

Some tolerations are hard to change; they're probably **facts**. So change your **attitude** to them instead.

attitude
positive mind

I tolerate	So
Expensive coffee in so called coffee bars	From now on, I'm only going to have it as a last resort.
My wife buying food that she and the kids like and forgetting what I want	I'm going to go shopping with her more often.
Late trains	When it happens, it's a **fact**. I'm just going to change my **attitude** towards it. I'll inform whoever I'm meeting immediately that the train is late (just in case one thing they tolerate is people telling them they're late just before they're supposed to arrive!) I'll also use the time I've gained to call somebody who I've not spoken to for a while and catch up with them. I'll do my parents first as they don't get enough of my attention when I'm working. I won't buy an expensive coffee just to kill time.

Regularly list what you tolerate.

Take time to quickly fix the things you tolerate.

If you can't fix what you tolerate, share it.

If it still can't be fixed, consider it a **fact** and change your **attitude** to it instead.

Reframing

Reframing involves taking something and altering it so that it means something different. If you decide to, you can reframe a negative comment to bring out the positive aspects.

Reframing allows you to take something that is an apparent obstacle and turn it into a positive. You can reframe your own **thoughts** and you can reframe other peoples' statements.

When you reframe, you immediately move from can't to **can**; from impossible to **possible**; from no-win to **must win**; from passive to **active**

I asked my wife recently to tell me something that she would like to change.

her statement	reframe
'I worry too much.'	Worrying is a great skill to have. Imagine if you didn't worry about anything at all; you would be completely carefree and may do some pretty rash things.

The reframe allowed her to consider a behaviour that she previously held as negative in a totally different way. It enabled her to realise that worrying is bad in certain **contexts** and good in others. She now knows that she doesn't have to worry about being worried.

attitude
positive mind

Reframing is a creative process. It demands that you consider things in different ways and **distort their context**.

A reframe is simply taking a **map of reality** and putting it in to a different dimension.

> "Shoot for the moon. Even if you miss, you'll land among the stars."
>
> **Les Brown**

Reframing a problem as a **positive outcome** is a really cool way to switch on your positive mind. Instead of focusing on the problem, you immediately focus on the possibilities of success.

statement	positive outcome reframe
I can't lose weight.	I will be 10 pounds lighter.

Which of these would motivate you to change your habits? Why do you think 'weight watchers' chose that name? Maybe they want customers to focus on their problems so that they continue to pay membership fees. I'm sure that 'toned bodies' would be a more positively reframed name.

statement	positive outcome reframe
Your son stares out of the window and daydreams in class.	Cool. He should make a really good inventor if his daydreaming skills are so advanced at this young age. How are you going to improve your teaching skills so that you interest him more?

Remember, if you don't **reframe things**, you'll never **see the positives**. If you fail to see the positives, you'll never **be exceptional**.

Anchoring

Have you ever heard a song and become emotional? Have you ever heard somebody use a certain voice tone that's made you feel tense or angry?

Have you ever sat in a specific room and felt completely relaxed and at ease? Is there a food or drink that makes you feel nauseous even if you just think about it?

These things are **anchors**. They are things in the real world that you've attached to internal **emotions**. Either by repetition or through the intensity of your emotions, you've unconsciously anchored the way you feel with these things.

It's useful knowing this for two reasons:

Firstly, you can accidentally anchor **negative emotions** to things that you see, hear and feel, emotionally and physically, every day.

You could anchor a difficult period at work with your drive home; even when work gets better, you'll somehow feel down as you experience the same anchors on the way home.

You could anchor frustration in a meeting with the chair you were sat in; sit in the same chair next time and you'll probably feel the same.

You could anchor playing badly in a game of squash with the socks you wore at the time. As you look down at them, you recall what it felt like last time you looked down each time you lost a point. Even if this time you're looking down at the floor for a different reason, you'll still recall some of that losing emotional **state**.

attitude
positive mind

Secondly, you can create your own anchors. You can **reinforce positive feelings** using the things around you that you hear, feel and see. When you re-experience the physical, your mind will automatically re-create the emotional.

To anchor a positive **state**, you need to identify a physical action that you can easily recreate such as pressing your finger and thumb together or scratching your earlobe.

Then, perform this action at the same time as you experience the feelings and thoughts that you want to anchor. You can even re-attach these feelings to the action each time you experience them to reinforce the anchor.

Then, whenever you want some of that emotional **state** back, simply perform the action again.

> Next time you realise that you're really good at something, look at your watch – but take time to notice the detail, the numerals the length of the hands, the colours and tones, even the scratches. Then hold the good feeling and touch your watch, making sure you get a specific texture or sensation. Finally, hold it to your ear and listen to the ticking or tap it and notice the sound it makes.
>
> This is a perfectly innocuous chain of events; you just look like somebody who is checking their watch. But it will allow you to automatically and unconsciously recall those good **emotions**. Better still, the more you do it, the stronger it gets.
>
> Just don't lose your watch.

how to be exceptional

If it sounds like hocus-pocus, call a hypnotist and ask them how they would go about curing a spider phobia. That is one of the most extreme examples of re-programming somebody's emotional response to physical stimuli.

Positive anchors are the opposite of phobias. You attach good feelings to objects and allow them to make you feel great when you experience them.

Just as people who are phobic of spiders get a certain emotion when they experience a spider, **your positive anchor gives you an automatic positive emotional state** when you experience whatever you anchored that state to.

There are a number of ways to cure phobias but the most common method uses anchors.

> Realise that there are things around you that you haven't even noticed with a curious ability to sap your positive attitude.
>
> Then, notice that there are other things around you that you can use to **capture your positive attitude** so that it can be released again whenever you need some of it.

attitude
positive mind

Beware infection

Most developed nations inoculate young children to prevent them from being infected by common but potentially lethal infections. It's a pity that we haven't yet developed an equivalent technology for inoculating ourselves from being infected by negative attitudes.

You probably already know that being aware of risk is important. But living your life in constant fear of risk is a sure-fire way to develop a negative attitude. So, there are two types of people that you should avoid at all costs; the **unhappy** and the **unlucky**.

If you spend too much time with **unhappy** people, you'll become one of them. In the same way that yawning is infectious, spending time with people who have a 'glass half empty' outlook will gradually wear you down too.

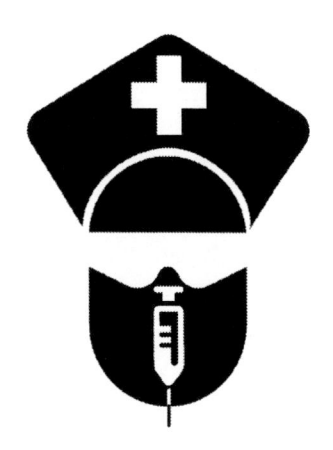

Go and sit on the Tube in London and have a look around. Excluding tourists who can just **reframe** their trip as a holiday, I could offer you £1 for every happy person you find.

2.6 million people travel the London Underground each day, so I'd be exposing myself to the tune of £930 billion over a year but I'm pretty confident.

They all look unhappy. They're unhappy because they've **anchored** negative feelings of delays and hot sweaty journeys with the carriage and the other unhappy people surrounding them.

how to be exceptional

> "We act as though comfort and luxury were the chief requirements of life, when all that we need to make us happy is something to be enthusiastic about."
>
> **Charles Kingsley**

Although there are plenty of ways of keeping the unhappy at bay, the safest form of protection is avoidance.

Be on your guard.

The **unlucky** are that way because they've decided to be. If you live your life following the mantra that you never have any luck and that nothing good ever happens to you, then you're probably right.

If your friends and colleagues walk around under a thundercloud, walk either ten paces behind them or ten paces ahead. Even if you walk behind them, you'll end up ahead at some point.

If you're unlucky, you stop taking risks. If you don't take risks, the chances of you becoming exceptional are remote.

> "Living at risk is jumping off the cliff and building your wings on the way down."
>
> **Ray Bradbury**

I'm not suggesting that you go around cutting the parachute strings of all your friends, family and workmates who occasionally bring you down. But once in a while, take a look around you at the people who are eating away your positive ambrosia and starve them of the luxury.

> Identify the people around you who sap your positive energy and distance yourself from them.
>
> Treat people who are constantly unhappy and unlucky as though they are lepers.

attitude
positive mind

Module 3 - Exercise

If you want an injection of positivity, immediately list ten things that you tolerate now.

Between now and the next module, do one of the following with each of your tolerations:

- **Fix** it. Do something so you no longer have to tolerate it.
- **Share** it. Discuss it with other people who either cause it or are impacted by it.
- Realise that it is a **fact** and change your **attitude** towards it.

how to be exceptional

awareness
strengths first

Module 4 : Strengths First

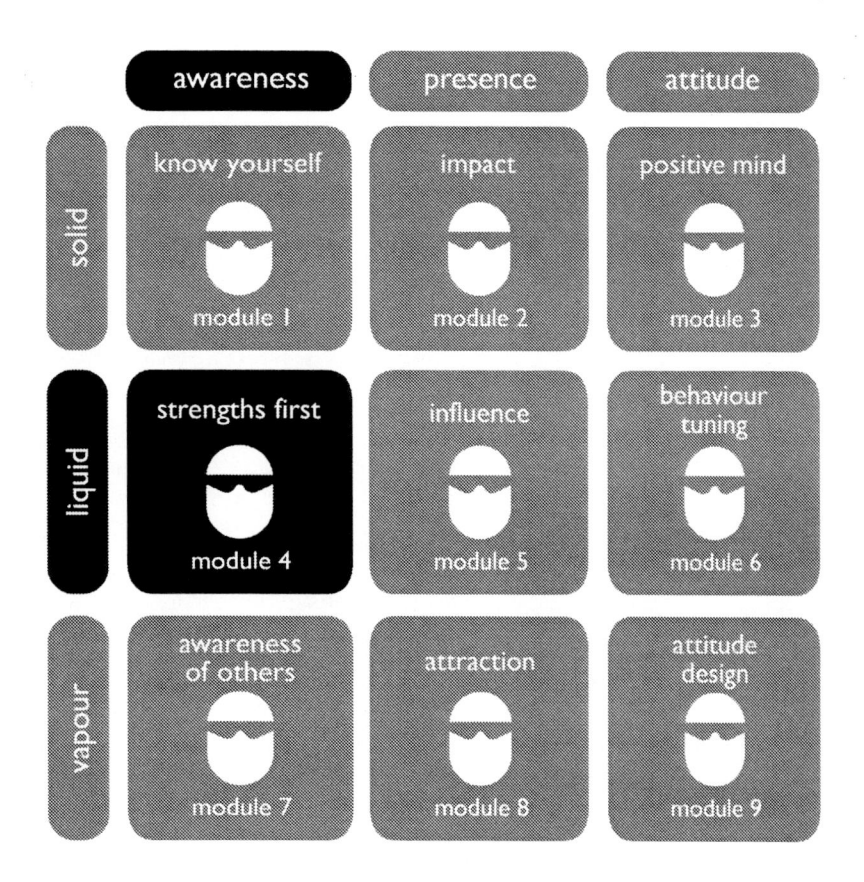

	awareness	presence	attitude
solid	know yourself module 1	impact module 2	positive mind module 3
liquid	**strengths first** **module 4**	influence module 5	behaviour tuning module 6
vapour	awareness of others module 7	attraction module 8	attitude design module 9

Most personal development programmes focus on identifying your weaknesses and then suggesting that you fix them.

In my **map of the reality**, this is nonsense. If you want to be more exceptional, you should find what you're good at and do more of it. Ditch the stuff you can't do; let other people do it.

Module 4 gives you the awareness that will kick start this process for you.

47

how to be exceptional

Tribal Archetypes

Psychometric tests are called that for a reason; they involve psychos coming along to measure you. They use an illogical cryptographic code to put you into a hallucinated box that allows other people to make sense of how you behave.

That way, you're personality, skills and flexibility can be put to one side so that you can be slotted into a perfect position on some perfect diagram.

The **Myers**-Briggs Type Indicator test was created in 1942. It classifies people into 16 groups depending on their bias towards:

Introvert vs. **E**xtrovert
Sensing vs. **I**ntuition
Thinking vs. **F**eeling
Judging vs. **P**erceiving

The **Belbin** model looks at typical team roles such as:

Shaper, Plant, Monitor Evaluator, Completer Finisher, Implementer, Resource Investigator, Team Worker, Chairman and Specialist.

As you might realise, I'm not a great believer in psychometrics as a means of assessing performance potential. In my **map of reality**, I'd like to think that as an evolved culture, natural selection has put us into more meaningful groups that have enabled us to survive and prosper.

Up until the last century, there was no Myers-Briggs or Belbin to guide how we understand ourselves but we didn't do too badly for 200,000 years.

Choose something on the edge of your comfort zone that you usually find to be a challenge and imagine for a moment that you're a Belbin *Completer Finisher*.

How much more confident do you feel knowing that somebody has decided for you that you can complete and finish things?

awareness
strengths first

I started to wonder how classification of peoples' behaviours used to work before this stuff was made up and I stumbled on a great piece of research.

In the book *Four-Fold Way*, Angeles Arrien studied Native American tribes and discovered that tribal culture was based on four archetypal roles that seemed to have been present in most ancient cultures.

She noted that tribes were made up of **Visionaries, Teachers, Healers** and **Warriors**.

Indigenous tribes expected their visionaries to **tell truth without blame or judgement**. People looked to these people for **direction** so that the tribe could survive and thrive.

Tribal teachers provided **clarity, objectivity, discernment and detachment**; they passed **knowledge** and customs to the younger generations so that the tribe had continuity of **purpose**. They were also comfortable with uncertainty and **trusted their inner knowledge**.

Source: The Four-Fold Way by Angeles Arrien

Tribal healers **paid attention to what has heart and meaning**. They were able to acknowledge the **feelings and emotions** of others and ensure that individuals and their inter-relationships were healthy.

Warriors were guided by the principle of **showing up and being present**. They **lived for the moment** and would willingly give their life to ensure the tribe survived. They showed **honour** and **respect; responsibility** and **discipline**.

how to be exceptional

When I first read this, I did what you're doing now. I went inside and thought 'I wonder which I would have been?'

Eventually, I realised that we all perform all of these roles in our workplaces, homes and communities today.

To me this is a really useful way to try and categorise peoples' behaviours. It's useful because you can remember it, relate to it and it allows you to be aware that people can float between roles:

- o of course the teacher will fight if he has to
- o of course the visionary will dream up new healing potions
- o of course the warrior will teach the young men how to fight

You and everybody around you have natural roles; they're what you do best. It could be that you're 80% of one role and 10% of two others, but there will be a natural balance for you.

Most importantly, you can get inside your roles if you want to and really begin to adopt their behaviours and principles.

> As you hear the frenzied battle cry of your tribe around you, feel the weight of your heavy rustic armour on your bruised and battered body. Take a moment to carefully inspect your weapons, making sure they're close at hand and primed. Look up at the marauding chaos ahead of you and take in a long deep breath.
>
> Now, consider that challenge.
>
> You're a Warrior – go and do battle.

awareness
strengths first

Don't let somebody else put you in a pigeon holed box that describes how you should behave according to their **map of reality**; decide what your natural role is first.

> "There is more to us than we know. If we can be made to see it, perhaps for the rest of our lives we will be unwilling to settle for less."
>
> **Kurt Hahn**

For the record, experts have told me that I'm an ESTJ and a Plant and I think that helped them more than it did me. But deep down, I know that I'm 70% Visionary, 20% Warrior, 10% Teacher and that I very rarely heal.

Know what you are naturally best at and consciously get in to character more often.

When you are with others, find the natural visionaries, teachers, healers and warriors and divide tasks and remits based on what they do best.

Get the visionaries to think, the teachers to educate, the healers to mend and the warriors to fight.

how to be exceptional

Journey to today

What you intend to do next is not part of your experience. What you have done is in the past is. During job interviews, most interviewers follow a format of walking though a candidate's career chronologically.

> "You can't build a reputation on what you're going to do."
>
> **Henry Ford**

The interviewer looks for parallels; examples where the candidate has done things similar in the past to the job that they're applying for now. People naturally assume that what you've done in the past is a yardstick for how you'll perform in the future.

The way that you explain your experience is an opportunity to make an **impact** and change the **state** of the people you're trying to **influence**.

People who can't describe what they have done in a way that makes it both **interesting** and **believable** unconsciously tell you that they're unexceptional.

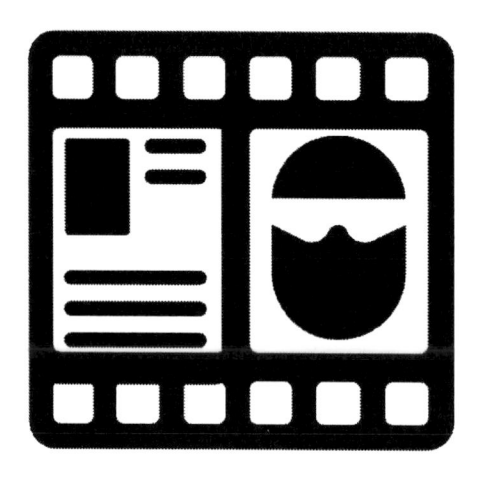

It's interesting how some people explain their **journey to today**. For some, it's an apologetic amble through job roles explaining their duties as bullet points.

For others, it's a megalomaniac's ego trip littered with responsibilities such as school prefect and under 8s football captain; and dizzy achievements like the highest O Level English Literature Exam mark in Derbyshire in 1979.

awareness
strengths first

There are hobbies and dependents, driving licences and interests, even photos and company logos.

The information **between the lines** is the most important part when you describe your journey to today. It's a **story**; a rich story of how you got to be where you are now. It has to explain your credibility and integrity and then lead **unconsciously** to where you want to go next. It has to flow smoothly and demonstrate what you have achieved **consistently**.

Above all, it has to be interesting.

> Think about the decisions on your **Journey to today** that represent key changes in direction or have been the differences that have made the difference.
>
> Notice that certain things could have happened that may have taken you in a completely different direction; events, decisions and relationships. What you did at these waypoints has made you who you are and brought you to where you are today.
>
> These waypoints become the chapters in your story. Like all good chapters, they begin with energy and end with anticipation of the next installment.

Don't be fooled into thinking that your journey to today is your CV. It's **any** opportunity you get to introduce yourself where you can tell a story that sells your value. Make no apologies if half the people in the room have heard it all before as you explain it to the people who don't know you; that will just serve to re-enforce it.

Be consistent and factual but don't be shy of name dropping companies and people.

> "To avoid criticism, do nothing, say nothing, be nothing."
>
> **Elbert Hubbard**

how to be exceptional

Don't be afraid to **reframe** your older experience differently if it can be used to underpin your current position. If you used to be a builder and are now a project manager; **reframe** what you built so that it uses project management cues - plan, build, on time, reputation and so on.

Outline you journey to today as a flow and use it to build your:

- CV
- elevator pitch
- meeting introduction script
- setting credibility statement
- chat up lines

Practice your story frequently and add to it as each chapter of your experience unfolds. Always be ready to impress people with your story; especially yourself.

Make it a $100m Hollywood blockbuster, not a second rate B-movie that came straight out on DVD.

awareness
strengths first

Welcome your weaknesses

As a culture in the West, we are conditioned in our development at home, school and work that our **weaknesses** are bad things. We are encouraged to find them and get better at them. In our early education, you can't fault this as an approach; if you can't write your name by five years old, then that's going to be an issue if it's not addressed. If you can't multiply a couple of years later, the same applies.

However, if you can't remember the dates of the Crimean War when you're 14, it's probably not a show stopper. If you can't generate new ideas quickly by the time you're 25, you're probably not naturally creative. If you can't plan an event in detail meaning that it runs smoothly and there are no surprises, you're probably not suited to being a project manager.

Many organisations have an approach to personal development that basically says:

> "Assess people against a list of what can be done by a human and find the things they aren't naturally as good at. Then, book training courses to try and get them to do the unnatural things that they aren't so good at better, even if they don't enjoy doing them."

This is why most organisations are full of unhappy, average, unexceptional people. Their talents are blended into a smoothie of mediocrity.

What's the alternative? How can personal development be more effective?

How about you **identify what you don't do naturally well** and bury it deep underground in a lead lined box?

how to be exceptional

Find other people who enjoy doing it and hence do it well. Then, with all the time you've created, **do more of the stuff you're good at** and enjoy.

Organisations call this 'outsourcing non core activity'.

So, **welcome your weaknesses and outsource your non-core activity**. Find other ways to get it done so that you do what you do best more of the time.

As soon as you welcome your weaknesses and focus fully on your strengths, you become **happier**, more **focused**, more **productive** and more **reliable**.

What you also find, as a by-product, is that you discover plenty of other enjoyable stuff to do in the extra time that you create for yourself by not doing the things that you're not good at.

> Identify your weaknesses and stop doing them.
>
> Outsource all the stuff you don't do well or don't enjoy and find other ways to get it done.
>
> Then, spend more time doing the things you enjoy and the things you do well. Invest your energy in these things and you will feel like you're freewheeling instead of peddling up hill.

awareness
strengths first

Failure vs. Feedback

There is no such thing as failure, only feedback. This is a really simple **reframe**. So simple in fact that it's easy to just say 'oh yes, I see' and move on. So **stop** for a moment, let me give you some **feedback** on why you have yet to fully understand what I mean.

Remember, **reframing** is changing the meaning of a statement so that it has a different impact. Reframing **Failure** as **Feedback** ensures that your **state** is not affected when you don't perform at your best. Being able to do this gives you greater strength and resolve.

If you fail a test, take the feedback that you need to practise more.

If you fail to win a sporting match, take the feedback that you didn't do certain things right in the game.

If you fail to get a job, take the feedback that it probably wasn't the right job for you.

> "If you fail, pay your helpers double."
>
> **Friedrich Nietzdche**

If you asked somebody to do something and they failed to deliver what you wanted, take the feedback that you could have explained what you wanted more accurately.

how to be exceptional

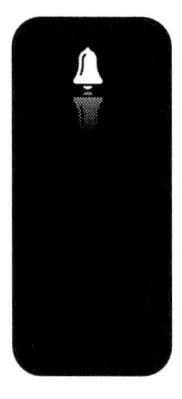

Remember a time when you were told that you failed.

You may have been told by somebody else or it may have been your own **self talk**.

Now, take what was said and change it from failure to feedback. Notice how you feel when you consider feedback instead of failure.

It's impossible to fail. It's only possible that you learn from how well you did and get better next time. As soon as you entertain the notion of failure, you're unexceptional

"If you want success, double your failure rate."

Tom Watson

If you're told that you failed, ask the person bringing the bad, incorrect news **'what's causing you to believe that I failed?'**

That's your feedback.

o **Failure** focuses on a **fact**
o **Feedback** focuses on your **attitude** to the fact

awareness
strengths first

Dos and Don'ts

Most people have clear notion of right and wrong. They know that certain things are good and others are bad because they've been conditioned to believe that certain things are or aren't appropriate.

In module 1, we discussed how you are **given your values**. They are difficult to change because you're attached to them at an emotional level.

But, we cannot simply accept that we have been conditioned to be who we are entirely by others. There must be a way to update your values based on the things you learn later in life.

> Imagine that you're taxiing in a plane. It is slowly moved into position at the start of the runway and you begin to feel the intense power of the engines as they spin up to full thrust. You gradually begin to move off the mark, gathering momentum as you accelerate along the runway. Your anticipation builds with the speed and noise until you gently lift off the ground.
>
> You're airborne.
>
> You gain height in the same way that you gather your **values** and sense of right and wrong throughout childhood and adolescence. At a certain point, you stop climbing.
>
> As you reach your cruising altitude, you adjust your settings and respond to the conditions outside and at 30,000 feet, you turn on autopilot.

how to be exceptional

Your life from 21 onwards isn't a routine flight from Heathrow to Glasgow.

There's more uncertainty and you have to make some pretty big adjustments along the way; tests, exams, interviews, jobs, partners, joint accounts, spouses, mortgages, sofas, children, pets, cars, promotions and demotions all fill the sky like foo-fighters.

You can **update your values with Dos and Don'ts** along the way.

Dos and **Don'ts** are the values that you decide to give to yourself in addition to those that you absorb from the World around you.

They are the things that you decide are **important enough** not to compromise so that you fly a safe course and reach your final destination.

my Don'ts	my Dos
Don't spend more that 8 nights per month away from my family. This is a pretty big issue as a management consultant.	Do give knowledge and time to people as it invariably repays itself in some way.
Don't take on work that you won't enjoy just because it's profitable.	Do spend time with the people that are important to you whenever you get chance.

I know people who have taken jobs by ignoring the things that are really important to them when they were interviewed. They have then been surprised three months later when they're unhappy at work.

awareness
strengths first

That's crazy if you **stop and think** about it for a second. People actually lie to themselves and then hope that the truth will be different from what they already believe to be true.

As I write this on a train ride back home from London, I've just met with a client who wouldn't employ me two years ago on a self-employed part-time basis because they needed a full-time person. I've just been asked back as an independent consultant to work on a project 3 days per week. Two years ago, I had two sacrosanct principles - **Don't** work away from my family and **Don't** take a permanent job. They served me well and are now paying for me to invest time teaching you to do the same.

Don't ignore things that you will later not be able to ignore; it's a recipe for stupidity. If you want to be exceptional, start with firm **Dos** and **Don'ts** as your basic ingredients.

> "Facts don't cease to exist because they are ignored."
>
> **Aldous Huxley**

If you live by your Dos and Don'ts, you'll be much happier.

You'll also be amazed how flexible people will be when you firmly state your Dos and Don'ts. If you tell people what you want, you're more likely to get it. If you keep it a secret, you'll be disappointed when you don't get it.

It really is that simple.

Stating your Dos and Don'ts allows you to **update your values with the things that are important to you now.**

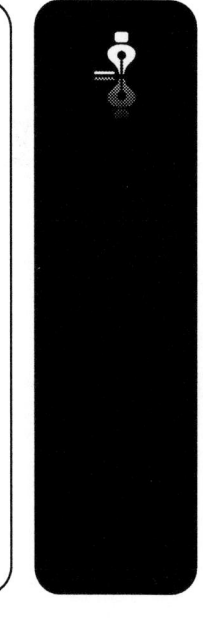

Module 4 - Exercise

You'll need to plan to spend at least two separate 30 minute sessions on this and ideally find an environment where you won't be interrupted.

Take the work you did at the end of module 1 where you **clarified** your **values**.

Update your values by adding the things that are important to you **now**, listing them in the form of **Dos** and **Don'ts**.

As you do this, refine your **Who I am** statement.

Make sure that it reflects your key **strengths** and the important and interesting points from your **Journey to today**.

By the end of this exercise, you will have:

- A set of clarified **values** updated with a set of current **Dos** and **Don'ts**
- A longer and richer **Who I am** statement

presence
influence

Module 5 : Influence

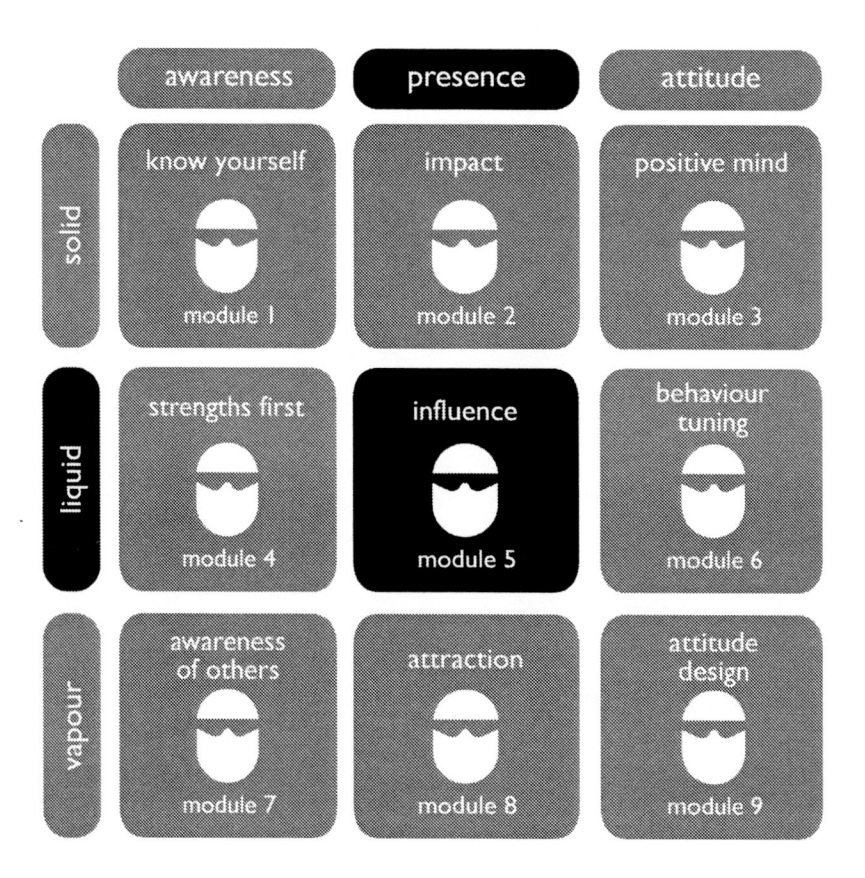

	awareness	presence	attitude
solid	know yourself (module 1)	impact (module 2)	positive mind (module 3)
liquid	strengths first (module 4)	**influence (module 5)**	behaviour tuning (module 6)
vapour	awareness of others (module 7)	attraction (module 8)	attitude design (module 9)

To be exceptional, you need to get the things that you want. Things like outcomes, job offers, decisions, respect and opportunities. To legitimately get the things that you want, you need to influence people. Influence involves ensuring that other people appreciate your views and agree with both their logic and their intent.

In module 5, you'll begin to appreciate some of the behaviours and patterns of language that make you more influential so that you become even more exceptional.

Rapport

How many times each day do you think about rapport? How many times each day do you break rapport with people around you? Do you ever consciously set out to build rapport?

Rapport is one of those rare qualities. Not rare in that it doesn't happen often, because it's everywhere and happening all of the time; but rare in that most people don't **consciously** consider it as they go about their lives.

There are no other words in our language that mean the same; the word is borrowed from the Old French *raporter* – meaning to bring back and the Latin word *portare* – meaning to carry. Its closest antonyms are **compatibility, resonance** and **accord**.

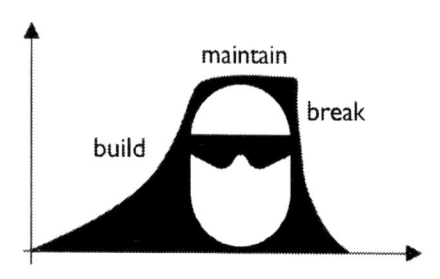

Rapport is a behavioural quality that either improves or diminishes the effectiveness of your communication.

Rapport can be built, maintained or broken.

Without rapport, you cannot influence. So in order to influence, you must know how to build and maintain rapport. Although you may not consciously use them, you already have skills in rapport building. Because rapport is usually unconscious, you don't always realise when you are failing to maintain rapport or, still worse, break it.

Broken rapport is hard to fix. If somebody breaks your rapport, it may take them longer to re-establish strong rapport with you. In some cases, they might never be able to regain your rapport at all.

presence
influence

Many books and theories on the subject have a golden rule that states 'never break rapport'. That's only a useful approach if you always want to have it. Sometimes, breaking rapport is the right thing to do if you want a certain outcome.

The golden rule I'd like you to consider is this:

Be constantly aware of the level of rapport that you have with the people you're communicating with.

> Many 'experts' over generalise rapport as body language and 'matching'.
>
> They will tell you that if you match somebody else's body language with your own, it will build rapport.
>
> For example, if you put your hand on your face, so will they. This may well be true but it isn't a very practical way to influence people. Why would you want to get somebody to put their hand on their face?

Factors affecting rapport include appearance, dress, body language, mannerisms, facial expressions and habits. There are also audible factors such as voice tone, pace of speech, choice of words, volume of voice, failure to listen and interruptions.

Many of the factors that affect the rapport that you build obviously depend on the preferences of the recipients of your communication and the **state** that they're in. However, you can't adjust all of your communication to cater for all of the factors that affect all recipients.

If you want to be exceptional, it's much simpler to ensure that you don't do things that break rapport with the majority of people – avoid the common mistakes. The simplest way of understanding these is to notice how other people break your rapport.

When somebody is talking to you, notice your internal **state**. When your state changes, identify what it was **specifically** that led to the change in rapport that led to a change in your state.

There is a universal principle that can be used to explain rapport breaks in many different contexts, be they cultural, managerial, technical or matrimonial; **empathy**. Good empathy is the basis of great rapport.

Because you have to **project yourself into other peoples' positions** in order to have empathy, you begin to notice things about yourself and what you're doing that builds, maintains or breaks rapport.

In module 7 we discuss **perception** in more detail and introduce a technique that can be used to build your empathy skills. Many of the topics covered later in the programme will give you additional positive ways to affect your rapport skills. Some have already been covered:

Maps of reality	Stating opinion as fact can break rapport because the recipient cannot relate to your map when theirs is different.
Transmit vs. Receive	Having to listen to somebody, who is 90% transmit and 10% receive, make a really long statement before you can have your say can break your rapport.
	Conversely, if you flip into 80% receive mode, it becomes a great rapport builder because people like to feel like they're being listened to.
Intensity x frequency	Low intensity, high frequency communication is a rapport breaker. Listening to the same people say the same thing in the same way is not a sound basis for rapport.

presence
influence

Become constantly aware of the level of rapport that you have with the people you're communicating with.

Build a mental catalogue of the things that you do when you break **rapport** with 'people'.

Gradually iron out the big rapport breakers from your own behaviour.

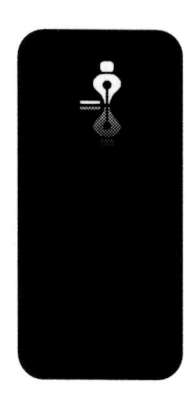

how to be exceptional

Being vague

The simplest way to break **rapport** is to say something that you believe to be true but which everybody around you disagrees with.

Specific information has a higher risk of breaking rapport than general information or no information at all.

The more people you're influencing at a given time, the more vague you should be since there will be a greater risk of breaking rapport with their combined **maps of reality**. Obviously, you can't converse totally content free but you should be wary of unnecessary content.

> Relax as I test your senses.
>
> Take in a deep breath of air through you nose and notice it fill your head and lungs with fresh oxygen. As you exhale slowly, I'm going to ask you to imagine that you hold out your hand as I place a freshly picked rose gently between your finger tips. You notice the fresh dew on the stalk as you carefully hold it, avoiding the perfectly formed pin sharp thorns. Raise it close to your nose and take in another deep breath through your nostrils and inhale the delicate natural perfume.
>
> That's right. Now watch the striking blue petals dance in wind as it blows across the bow of the boat.

At which point did I break rapport? I'd imagine it was when I gave very specific information; especially specific information that was different to that which you were creating in your mind as I led you with words.

presence
influence

If I'd have said 'white petals' I'd have broken rapport if you were imagining a red rose. If I'd said 'red petals' I'd have broken rapport if you were imagining a white rose.

So blue was going to blow you out of the water either way. Just for good measure, I placed you in a specific place (on a boat) that was highly likely to be different to the one that you were imagining.

Since I've known about being vague, I've used the word **certain** more than ever. Not in the context of 'being certain in my mind' but to relate to a measure or quantity of something that is as yet undecided.

Consider the following statements in the context of me trying to establish with somebody that a piece of work should be split into two separate phases:

We'll spend three weeks on the first phase before we move on to the second.	In this case, 'three weeks' is a potential rapport breaker if all I'm trying to do is establish that we'll have two phases. In a certain person's mind, they may have already decided that it will be three days or three months – and I'll break rapport with them.
We'll spend a certain amount of time on the first phase before moving on to the second.	In this case, I'm not likely to break rapport over a vague time period but I can still establish that there will be at least two phases.

This has its place. Sometimes, detail is exactly what's required. However, if you don't need detail, then don't use it.

Specific information has a higher risk of breaking rapport than general information or no information.

To test for unnecessary content, ask yourself:

1. Will the point I'm making be roughly the same without it?

    o   Does it **really** add anything?

2. Is there a risk that somebody I'm making the point to will have a different opinion of the point because of it?

    o   Is it a **potential rapport breaker**?

If the answer is **yes** to both, then either remove the unnecessary content or replace it with something vague. You'd be amazed how willing the human mind is to make up its own content if it is correctly led.

In the rose example, something like this would do:

"…watch the silky petals dance before your eyes and gaze beyond them as you notice your surroundings…"

presence
influence

Principles vs. Specifics

Because you already have **context**, you understand the things that you describe to other people. But the people you're communicating with may not necessarily have the same understanding.

It's as though the things that you say are the visible parts of an iceberg, sticking out above the water. The true meaning of your communication may be hidden from view beneath the surface.

The language that people choose to use becomes a filter, creating the difference between what they actually say and what they really mean.

Sometimes, people can either be too detailed or too **vague** and you may need to **influence** them to adjust their **map of the reality** so that they consider how to communicate their meaning in a different way.

You may have come across the terms **chunking up** and **chunking down**, meaning to take a higher level perspective and to dig down into the detail.

There are some pretty cool techniques that you can use to get people to become more detailed or vague in their thinking.

Principles
chunk up

I have found these to be invaluable in situations where there is some form of disagreement or negotiation.

Specifics
chunk down

Asking somebody for the **principle** behind what they are saying forces them to become vaguer. When asked for a principle, most people follow a mental process something like this:

- Go inside and find other examples of the thing I'm thinking about

- Find a general name that can be given to all these things together

They then respond with a principle that is the unsaid **why** beneath what they initially said.

statement	principle
'I want a 5% pay rise in January.'	'I want more money.'

As soon as you get to a principle, it allows you to look for other ways to achieve the same principle. Why not leave and get a job somewhere else, re-skill yourself in something more lucrative or work overtime?

Principles are powerful because they allow you to gain agreement to the principles themselves instead of the specifics beneath them. When you get this, you can move forwards and **influence**.

'OK, I'll agree to help you find a way of getting you more money'

At other times, certain people may ask for something that they haven't thought through fully or they may offer a **vague response** when asked for detail. In many cases, these people know what they want but choose to use **vague language** when asking for it.

The word **specifically** embedded into questions works wonders here.

presence
influence

> Consider the following:
>
> 'The project is running late and we are going to miss our deadline.'
>
> **Reframe:** It's good that we know that we're going to be late this early...
>
> o How late are we **specifically**?
> o By how long **specifically** are we going to miss our deadline?
> o Which deadline **specifically**?
> o In fact, which project **specifically** are we talking about?

There are two reasons why **specifics are important**:

1. They get people to go inside and re-state what they said in more **specific** detail.

2. They ensure that all parties are actually talking about the same **specific** thing.

There are some big watch words that should be your alarm signals to go and pull out specifics.

Terms that generalise individuals	
they, we, he, she, us, people, the team, the management	Who **specifically** are we talking about?

Terms that generalise entities

it, the project, the company, the system, the competition	What **specifically** are we talking about? Which one **specifically** are we talking about?

Terms that generalise quantities or frequency

all, every, never, always	How often **specifically** does this happen? When **specifically** does this happen?

> Train your mind to spot where you and the people around you hide detail. If there is a risk that the lack of detail will reduce your ability to influence, ask for specifics.
>
> Equally, when you get bogged down in detail and cannot move forward, ask for principles that you can agree on before looking for alternative ways to agree details.

presence
influence

Unconscious influence

There's a **principle** that says 'you cannot not communicate'. It's a convoluted way of saying that **you are communicating all of the time, even when you don't think that you are**.

Because it's so easy to innocently and accidentally incorporate unconscious communication into your everyday language, you've probably unconsciously influenced people without even knowing it

Imagine what you could do if you decided to really **give it a try**.

If you have ever been around a crying child when their parent is trying to calm them down, you're likely to hear the parent say something like 'Come on, don't cry'. In order to tell the child not to cry, you have to also tell the child to cry. What the child hears are the words **come, on, don't** and **cry**.

There is a strong likelihood that the child will actually interpret **CRY** as an instruction to do just that. Since children are used to hearing and obeying instructions from their parents, they will do as they are told and cry more. Most children hear everything except the **don't** part.

Don't **drop your drink**, Don't **go into the house with your shoes on**, Don't **eat crisps in the living room**, Don't **leave your toys all over your bedroom**.

how to be exceptional

It's interesting that the most frequently used way to tell somebody not to do something involves telling them to do it at the same time. If you want to stop a child crying, tell them to laugh. You can even tell them not to laugh – both work with a greater success rate than saying 'don't cry'.

Much of what I'm about to get you to **learn now** has origins in hypnosis. I'd be worried if **you are** anything but **comfortable with this** because hypnosis is just an advanced form of influencing.

I don't expect you to **use this in the near future**. But I do want to make sure that **you're more aware** that there is much more to the way that you communicate with people than **you have noticed** until **now**.

Pacing and Leading

One of the fastest hypnotic inductions (this is how hypnotists get people into the **state** that, in their **map of the reality**, is called a trance) involves pacing and leading. In its simplest form, you **pace** by stating a number of factual things. Then you link them to something that you want to **lead** people to believe.

> I know that there is a lot of information here but as you relax in your surroundings, just notice the pace of your breathing and take a look around you at the colours where you are now. Choose a colour that you prefer most and begin to decide how you will use the information here tomorrow. It will probably be the second or third person who you use it with that will give you the most success. You just need to use factual things to establish the right level of **rapport**, be **vague** enough not to break it and then make your point.

presence
influence

You could imagine a simple form of this if you were doing a presentation. You might tell people where they are (*pacing with a fact*) by way of a welcome, you could then thank the people around you who spoke before or introduced you (*pacing with a fact*), you may show a brief slide explaining why you are there (*pacing with more facts*) and then you would tell them (*beginning to lead*) whatever you want them to believe in your presentation.

The basic equation for pacing and leading goes something like this:

> fact... fact... fact... tenuous fact...
>
> **your point**

I'm not suggesting that you'll put people into a trance and they'll believe whatever you say. I'm suggesting that people are more likely to respond to your suggestions if you pace and lead using this technique.

Talking in Quotes

You already know how effective stories are as a way of conveying information and, in module 2 - **intensity x frequency**, we covered the importance of stirring emotions when you communicate. So, one of the easiest ways of unconsciously installing an emotion into a person or group of people is to **talk in quotes**.

If you come straight out with a direct command such as **'you need to get your act together'** it is both hard for you to deliver and easy for you to break **rapport** with people.

However, if you were to tell a story about somebody else who you gave the direct command to, you could say exactly the same words to your recipients but deliver them in a different context.

how to be exceptional

You could even flip the quote so that you were the person being told to **'get your act together'**.

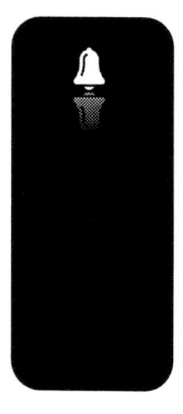

> The first time that I taught this to somebody they just didn't get it. So I said to them **'when you're relaxed in bed tonight, just mull over how easy it would be to embed a direct command into a sentence.'**
>
> They just looked at me blankly so I don't know whether they did it. I don't suppose you'd ever really know if you were to **think about this when you are sleeping**.

> Pace and lead people by using facts to establish **rapport** before introducing the things that you would like them to believe.
>
> Use quotes to deliver information without it sounding like it was delivered by you.
>
> **There's more going on than you realise. When you realise, you can make more go on.**

presence
influence

Hot / Cold & Push / Pull

We each have our own natural style of influencing others. Although we may vary our style in different situations, we tend to return back to a natural style that feels right.

Being aware of the different modes of influence is important, partly so that we know why what we do naturally doesn't always work and partly to enable us to build a broader influencing repertoire.

When we influence, we operate primarily in two dimensions; pressure and temperature:

Pressure	**Push vs. Pull**	We either push what we want to influence towards the people we're influencing, or we pull them towards our position.
Temperature	**Hot vs. Cold**	We are either warm and engaging or cold and distant. We sell or we tell.

Each of these modes can be combined to offer 4 different influencing styles.

Cold Push	Hot Push
Cold Pull	Hot Pull

Bridging
Cold Pull

When you do this, you bridge across to the people you're influencing; making sure that they know that you understand them. If somebody feels that they're being listened to, they're easier to influence – it is a huge **rapport** factor.

Bridging involves adopting an open posture to show that you're listening actively. It means exploring and asking questions that get people to open up and tell you what they really think, how they feel and why they feel the way they do.

Uncover peoples' beliefs through **bridging** questions like 'what makes you believe that?' or 'how do you know that's correct?'

You build strong bridges because people love to speak their mind and tell you how they feel.

> To bridge, you need to use open questions such as 'so…. tell me about what you're thinking' instead of closed questions that can be responded to with a simple yes, no or worse, a shrug.
>
> To really polish your bridging, summarise and reflect what you've heard people say. Acknowledge what you have observed so that people are more confident that you understand their perspective.
>
> Summarise their **facts** and reflect their **emotions**.

presence
influence

Persuasion
Cold Push

Persuasion is communication that has been designed to induce belief or action in people.

It's important to understand peoples' beliefs before you persuade them; so that you are more aware of possible objections. So use **bridging** questions first to establish their beliefs.

Then, when you know enough, you **use cold push to persuade**.

Persuasion is about getting other people to first understand and then agree with your perspective. You put forward your own position to people in a clear way and back it up with facts. Make firm, direct, decisive statements and ensure that they are based on fact as well as experience and opinion.

> Key factors in persuasion are controlling your **state** and being consistent. In the wrong state, persuasion can become argument.
>
> A lack of consistency will demonstrate weaknesses in the facts you present and will undermine your position.
>
> You must also **pace and lead** to effectively persuade others. This ensures that the facts that people do not yet agree with are combined with facts that they already agree with in order to make them more agreeable.

Assertion
Hot Push

If you want to be **assertive**, use hot push. This involves clearly stating your expectations and putting in place **pressures** or **incentives** that are meaningful to the people you're being assertive to.

There's little point in setting a pressure or incentive that doesn't have a connotation of 'pain or gain'. If there is a risk of a 'so what' response, change your pressures and incentives.

When you push, you must be clear not to confuse assertion with politeness. Assertion says **what you want** whereas politeness says **what you'd like**.

A useful pattern for constructing assertive statements:

What I want you to do is…	**…outcome**
I want you to do it in the following way…	**…style & specifics**
If you do it, you will get…	**…incentive**
If you don't do it, I will apply…	**…pressure**

What I want you to do is **re-read this page**. When you do it, I want you to **take your time and absorb the information fully**.

If you do it, **you'll be able to get more of what you want in life**. If you don't, **certain people may stop you getting the things you deserve**.

presence
influence

Attraction
Hot Pull

When you perform hot pull influencing, you attract people. You make them feel excited and important. **Attraction** involves describing a **future state** that people find desirable.

We cover specific attraction models in module 8. Until then, here are a few attraction tips that are worth introducing to you influencing style.

Build strength in others. Telling other people that they have done a great job and giving recognition is one of the most powerful forms of Hot Pull. Receiving compliments makes people want to be with you more. When people want to be with you more, they are more open to influence.

Disclose information. Telling other people information that is privileged makes them feel more important. This can either be personal disclosure, which will draw them closer to you, or more general information.

Giving away information that is about to enter the general public domain just before it's available forewarns them of things before they happen, and is a simple way of **attracting** them even more.

You don't need to tell people your inner-most secrets, just disclose appropriate information routinely and you will attract them.

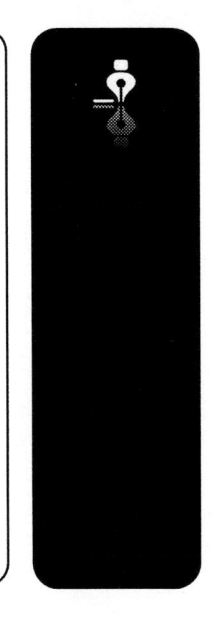

I once had a team working for me do something that I can only describe as heroic. They pulled out all of the stops against not only the odds but against the belief of everybody around them and delivered something that was close to unachievable. They were good, although not great, people. I made sure that they knew that they were good; I was **building strength**.

But I put their success down to **disclosure**.

A week before what we did was due to hit the most difficult period, I told them all that I was really worried. In fact, I told them that I thought that there was only a 50% chance we'd succeed. I talked for 10 minutes or so about how I felt and where my personal stress was with the things I had to deliver. I then had them all disclose how they felt.

In an hour, we created a team bond strong enough to pull us through anything that would face us.

Attraction is one of the most common influencing styles that I have witnessed exceptional people use. Exceptional people don't just attract people to them; they also attract people to each other and towards their vision of the future.

In my **map of reality**, it's so important that I've dedicated the whole of module 8 to it.

presence
influence

Module 5 - Exercise

As you recap the influencing models in module 5, you will notice that there are certain things that stand out as things that you do less than others.

Using this information, write down what you believe to be your natural influencing style.

Then, write down the influencing techniques that you are going to use next to complement your natural style and begin to identify where you can practice these techniques.

how to be exceptional

attitude
behaviour tuning

Module 6 : Behaviour tuning

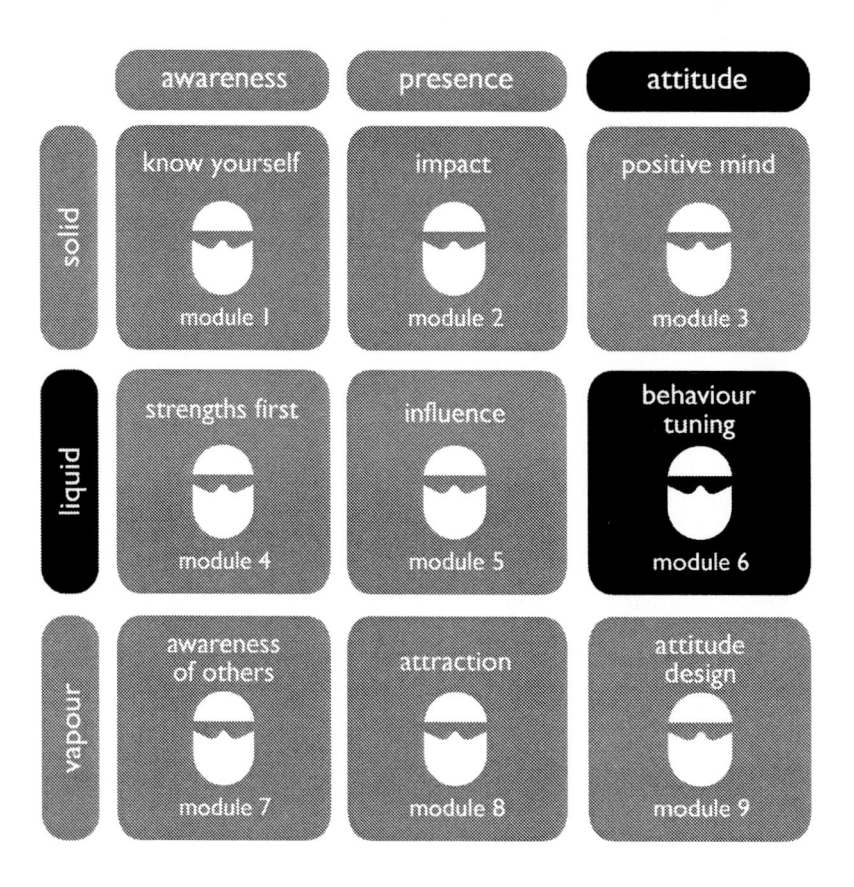

	awareness	presence	attitude
solid	know yourself	impact	positive mind
	module 1	module 2	module 3
liquid	strengths first	influence	**behaviour tuning**
	module 4	module 5	**module 6**
vapour	awareness of others	attraction	attitude design
	module 7	module 8	module 9

If you want a high performance car, you tune it. If you want a musical instrument to sound harmonious, you tune it. If you want to listen to a radio without annoying hiss and crackle, you tune it.

If you want your behaviour to enable you to be exceptional, you tune it.

You can use module 6 as your behavioural tuning fork.

how to be exceptional

Bullet time

Have you ever watched the Matrix movies? If you have, you'll remember the scenes where Neo slows down time so that he can dodge bullets fired at him by his adversaries.

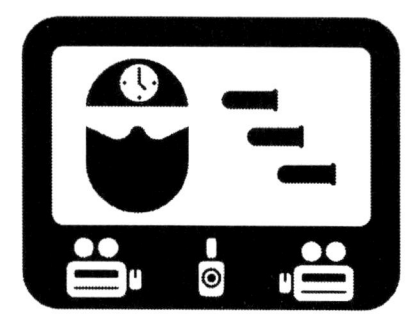

In certain scenes, motion freezes and the camera rotates around the subject as he is seemingly stationary in mid air, about to deliver a lethal martial arts style kick.

This is bullet time.

Although this cinematography technique isn't unique to the Matrix, it probably came to prominence in that movie.

Just as other film makers have copied the technique since, I'd like to suggest that you copy it routinely as part of whatever it is that you do. It's only when you manage to slow everything around you down that you **begin to really notice things**. You will notice things with your senses that previously passed you by.

Find two objects the same colour where you are now.

Notice the difference in shade between them. Notice how they reflect light differently, how their textures differ, what their temperature difference would be if you touched them. Then, notice the sensation at the back of your knees and how your tongue feels as you run it along your teeth.

attitude
behaviour tuning

We can focus our five senses in different ways. We can notice **internal** things that occur inside us. We can notice **external** things that happen around us. We can decide to focus our attention in a **narrow** band on very specific things. We can choose a **broad** focus on general themes.

Background noise as you walk down a street	Broad External focus
The feeling of a thumb nail on your first finger	Narrow Internal focus
Noticing the ambient light where you are	Broad External focus
Listening to the tone of your **self talk** voice	Narrow Internal focus

When you force yourself into **bullet time** you will notice more and become more sensitive to the things that you're doing. You take yourself out of your current activity and observe the small behavioural steps that make it up. The detail you notice allows you to fine tune your behaviour.

The first step in tuning your behaviour is noticing more than you do now.

Periodically, as you do things, choose to go into your own **bullet time**.

Slow everything down and notice more. Notice your **state** first. Once you've noticed that, take your time to notice the things that you don't usually notice. Go internal and external; narrow and broad. Notice more.

Take your findings and use them to tune what you do more precisely.

how to be exceptional

Congruence

Congruence is the quality that makes you convincing. It is that which provides those around you with the evidence they need in order to know that you're true to your communication. It's the billboard that you use all of the time to advertise who you really are.

Since **you cannot not communicate**, everything that you say and do, even the things you don't say and do, speak volumes about your feelings and understanding.

The language patterns that you choose to use and the slight behavioural cues that you're not even aware of provide people with a constant stream of unconscious information.

Incongruent people exhibit 'hypocritical' behaviour that belies their stated **values** and makes them appear unconvincing.

When did you last have your hair cut by somebody with terrible hair?

You need to **be congruent to be exceptional**. If you're not, people don't believe you at an **unconscious** level.

Worryingly, if it's unconscious, people don't even know at the time that they don't believe you – they just get a nagging feeling that something isn't quite right about you.

> "Act the part and you will become the part."
>
> **William James**

attitude
behaviour tuning

I was once working in an unfamiliar city and had to order some colour flyers from a print shop. I'd sent my artwork via e-mail an hour earlier when I walked in to the **Colour Copy Centre** and handed over my credit card to pay for the small run of prints. The proprietor impressed me – he noticed I was a new customer and proceeded to tell me what services the **Colour Copy Centre** offered. He boasted that they had invested in the latest print technology and could print up to a huge A0 size onsite. They could print onto vinyl allowing customers to produce striking banners that could be used on windows or vehicles and removed without marking surfaces.

I was impressed; so impressed that I asked for his price list. He handed me an A5 booklet with an image of a child wearing face paint in the style of a circus clown. Across the image was a strap line – **'an eye for detail & colour'** looking stylish in varying font sizes to accentuate the words **eye, colour** and **detail**; perfect. Perfect except the price list was in black and white and was a photocopy of a photocopy of an original. It had everything but colour and detail. Despite their impressive capability and sales style, I never returned.

If a colour copy centre can't take an appropriate level of pride in the one thing that represents the value for money of their own services, why should I **unconsciously** take them seriously?

I recently fished out the scanned copy of the pricelist that I keep as an example of incongruence. I typed in the website URL printed on it to see if they had a similar level of online incongruence. They had printed the wrong URL (a .com instead of a .co.uk).

The height of incongruence is a print shop with typographical errors on their own literature.

how to be exceptional

Being congruent requires that you examine your **personal style** and **identify** things that undermine your credibility. Congruence demands that you go into **bullet time** and become introspective.

No matter how polished you are, you will not be exceptional if the things that accompany the things that you do just don't **stack up** at an **unconscious** level.

Unconsciously, if they don't stack up; we don't believe you.

You could suffer from incongruence in your behaviour, appearance, ethics, values, marketing, gestures, voice tone or choice of response to others.

Even the throw away comments that you sometimes make provide people with all the information they need to disbelieve you.

Go into **bullet time** and notice the things you do that are incongruent with what you are trying to achieve. Look for the little tells that make you less credible because **your unconscious actions are contradicting your conscious intent**.

Consider congruence as a key factor in building **rapport**. Observe others for their incongruent traits and then iron them out of your own behaviour.

Design your own congruent behaviour that is consistent with your:

- **values**
- **who I am** statement
- **dos** and **don'ts**

attitude
behaviour tuning

Head vs. Heart

Making choices and decisions is a key aspect of our behaviour. At one end of the spectrum, people can be risk averse and will adopt a considered approach, choosing to think through the possibilities fully before deciding on a course of action. At the other extreme, people may be more comfortable with risk and will make fast impulsive decisions based on their gut instincts.

Neither is right or wrong but both methods have their place. Big decisions usually warrant thought. Opportunistic decisions often warrant agility.

Part of your decision making processes should not only include making the decision itself but, before you commit, you should also consciously consider how you made the decision. Was it using your **head** or your **heart**?

When you use your **head**, you're **logical** and **rational**. You apply **common sense** and look for facts that support your decision. You may also consider the **ecological** impact of your actions; 'if I do this, what else might happen?'

When you use your **heart** to make decisions, it usually **feels right** because it fits well with your **values**. There will be a larger **emotional** element to your decision, either based on your own **state** or because you have interpreted the **emotions** of the people involved or impacted.

Taking a more rounded view when making decisions ensures that you consider different perspectives before acting. Remember the **TEA model** in module 1 – **thoughts** from your **head** and **emotions** from your **heart** affect your **actions**.

how to be exceptional

But, there's a risk that you may jump straight in from an emotional perspective without applying the necessary thought rigour.

> Bookmakers understand that supporters of sports clubs think almost entirely with their heart when it comes to their own team. Often, supporters ignore their **head** when looking at **facts** such as odds that are stacked against their team and choose to follow their **heart** in believing that they can overcome the odds.

Training yourself to change your decision making processes requires that you go into **bullet time**. Pause the movie for a moment and move the camera around the decision that you're looking at, notice the stuff that you don't usually notice as you look from different angles.

When you've noticed enough, rewind and roll the film again.

> Whenever you are in the process of making a decision, go into **bullet time**. This is not something that you do after you **make decisions**; do it **during the process.**
>
> Ask yourself 'am I making this with my **head** or my **heart?**'
>
> Once you have your answer, ask yourself 'How would my decision differ if I made it from the other perspective?'
>
> This intervention takes a couple of seconds but often gives you additional insight that allows you to **tune** the decision or the way in which you communicate it to people involved and impacted.

attitude
behaviour tuning

Away vs. Towards

Because making decisions is a key behavioural trait, it's crucial that you understand why you're making them. Poor decisions are often made when you're trying to avoid or move away from your present situation. This is because you haven't focused on a positive outcome and therefore can't choose actions that support your destination.

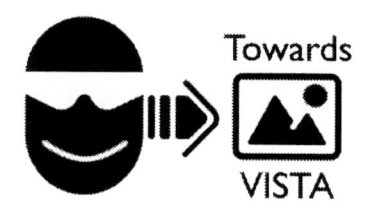

Imagine deciding to go on holiday and just packing a bag and walking out of your house. You'd pack some clothes but probably not the right ones. You'd set off and begin your journey without knowing where you were heading or how long it would take. When you arrived, you wouldn't know if that was your destination or somewhere along the way. Certain travel options wouldn't be viable or efficient so you'd spend much of your time planning and waiting instead of relaxing or enjoying. I can imagine that this type of holiday would have an appeal to a certain group of people but it isn't a great blueprint for most holidays.

You're either moving away from something or towards something. To move **away** from something, all you need is a **negative state**.

To move **towards** something, you need to **decide**, either **in principle or specifically, what you want**.

If you make decisions by moving away from something, you're more likely to end up in another place that you want to move away from. You become an **emotional hobo**; needing to move on constantly in order to become content.

how to be exceptional

> **AWAY thinking:**
>
> "I hate my job. I want to leave."

In my **map of reality**, you'll be happier and more successful if you **move towards things that you want** and not away from the things that you don't want.

There is a risk here though. If you're too specific with what you're moving towards you may find that either:

o You get disappointed when you arrive and it isn't quite what you expected

o You didn't know enough about what you wanted when you set off and therefore couldn't decide on a detailed enough destination

Always make decisions on the basis of moving towards something instead of away from something. Just **don't be too specific in your destination.**

> When people are desperate to leave a job they hate, the first thing they do is write a CV. Desperation isn't a great **state** to be in when writing a CV.
>
> Remember your **journey to today** – it needs to lead somewhere. It needs to **pace and lead** in a direction that is both your own preferred route and credible to the people who can take you there.

attitude
behaviour tuning

You may have come across **SMART** objectives. Countless organisations and development programmes use them, asking you to set objectives that are **S**pecific **M**easurable **A**chievable **R**ealistic and **T**ime-bound.

I've found that many extremely capable people fail to achieve their so called SMART objectives because they find them frustrating, stifling and pointless.

Instead, exceptional people set **VISTA** objectives. Their objectives are **V**ague **I**ntangible **S**tretching **T**angential and **A**head.

SMART	VISTA
Specific goals presuppose that it's possible to be precise and finite at the start of a journey.	**V**ague goals allow movement towards an outcome with the flexibility to change **specific** focus along the way.
Measurable goals require knowledge of the solution before it's defined. You can't measure what you don't know.	**I**ntangible goals improve confidence as every minor achievement along the way counts toward the outcome.
Achievable goals suggest that it's not necessary to improve beyond your current ability.	**S**tretching goals push the envelope of ability and possibility. They make you do more than you think you can.
Relevant goals assume that relevance to what you currently know will be best for you in the future.	**T**angential goals create the need to consider alternative directions that might be more useful than the usual way. They provoke change.
Time-bound goals frustrate people who miss deadlines and cause those who are ahead of the game to slow down.	**A**head goals can be achieved in one hour or a lifetime. They provide beacons, not destinations.

how to be exceptional

> **TOWARDS / VISTA thinking:**
>
> "I will work less and earn more in the future by doing things that fit more closely with my personal values."

You can also **influence** others to become more **specific** using towards thinking. When you are confronted by people who articulate their needs and wants in terms of what they don't want, you can use a simple **reframe** and say 'OK, I think I understand what you **don't** want, but can you tell me what you **do** want?'

Towards thinking is a great way to diffuse negative emotions such as complaints or crisis situations. Simply ask the person who is in the process of complaining 'So, how will you know that you're satisfied? What will I have to have done in order to make you happy again?'

You'll notice confusion on certain peoples' faces as they go inside and ask themselves the question and realise that they don't actually know.

In both situations you need to do two things:

Ask for positive evidence	What are you looking for?
	How will you know you have it?
Future pace it	State it in a time in the future.

When you future pace objectives, use words that presuppose that they're going to happen.

Don't say that you'd **like** to have a bigger house, say **when** you have a bigger house.

attitude
behaviour tuning

Don't say **if** something happens, you'll celebrate. Say that the **first time** it happens, you'll celebrate. First presupposes there will be a second, third and possibly hundredth time.

> Instead of running **away** from negative things, drive **towards positive** things. Set **VISTA** goals to drive your decisions.
>
> Although a **vague towards** goal isn't a **specific** destination, it's a much more useful mantra when making decisions than moving away from something.
>
> It's also easier to define and act upon than a traditional SMART objective.
>
> Use **evidence** to describe what your desired objective will be like and **future pace** it in **positive** words that presuppose that it is going to happen.

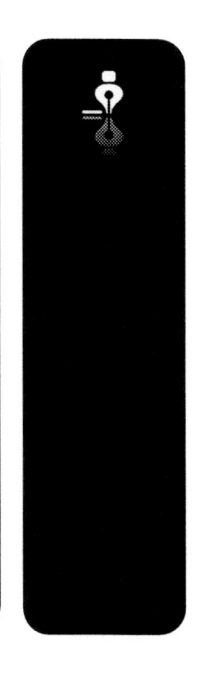

Intuiting to action

Closely related to the **heart** part of your decision making mind is your intuition. I've observed many people use their intuition since I became interested in the subject so I'd like to share my **map of reality** with you.

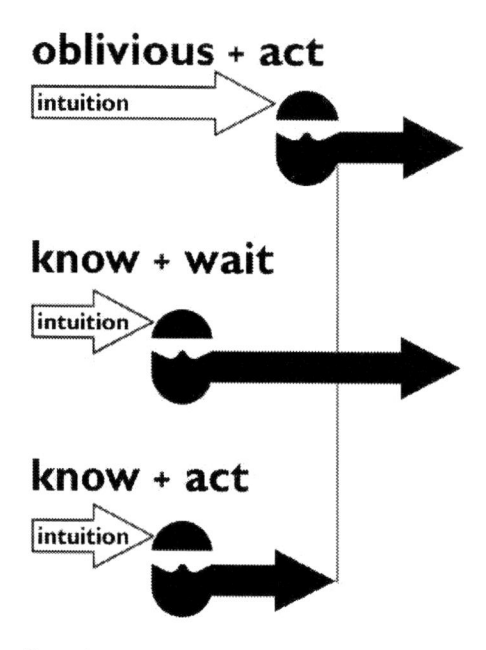

oblivious + act

intuition

When people choose a course of action, they often base it on their intuition.

know + wait

intuition

I don't think that people have natural ways of using their intuition but I do think that people use intuition differently depending on the context of a situation.

know + act

intuition

Things like stress, confidence and certainty are factors I believe affect the use of intuition.

I've observed people use three different strategies when intuiting.

Oblivious + Act

At times, people don't apply their intuition at all. They amble along doing whatever it is that they do until a point in time when they realise that a drastic course of action must be taken. They suddenly jolt into action and sprint for the finish line, getting there just about on time. There's usually a show of external stress right at the crescendo before an autopsy to find out what went wrong.

attitude
behaviour tuning

Know + Wait

At other times, people apply their intuition very early. They get a feeling that something different must be done to avoid some later obstacle. But, they wait; they fail to trust their intuition and mull things over in their mind.

They build up stress internally as they try to decide whether to share their concerns and if so, who with. They know what needs to be done much earlier than when they are in 'Oblivious + Act' mode but they sit on things for longer. At some point, they share their pent up concerns, get permission to act and then rush to the finish line just in time, albeit this time with a well rehearsed plan of action that they've worried about all along.

Know + Act

The most effective use if intuition I've observed is a predictable combination of the best parts of these two suboptimal strategies. Sometimes, people use and fully trust their intuition. As soon as they identify that something different must be done, they act immediately. There may be a short lag as the decision of 'what has to be done' is made using both **head** and **heart** as they move **towards** their destination, but the transition from **intuition** to **action** is smooth and fast.

Using this mode, **you will see obstacles sooner** and **act quickly**. You also tend to finish whatever it is that you're doing well before the **Oblivious Actors** and the **Knowing Waiters**.

There's less stress because you're confident in your thinking and on top of your action.

You could even spend more time on the action part and achieve a much better quality of outcome.

> "The only real valuable thing is intuition."
>
> **Albert Einstein**

how to be exceptional

If you had a sixth sense, it would probably be intuition. You consciously see, hear, feel, smell and taste. So I suggest that you **begin to consciously intuit**. Use your intuition as a sense and learn to trust it fully.

> When you do things, balance your intuition and action.
>
> Go into **bullet time** and consciously use your **intuition**. Trust it fully, asking both your **head** and **heart** for their input.
>
> When you **decide to act**, be **congruent** so that you are decisive and confident. Act with certainty.

attitude
behaviour tuning

Module 6 - Exercise

Create an **anchor** for your own **bullet time**.

Find a way to slow down your surroundings and notice more than you usually would. Each time you do this, use you anchor to re-enforce it.

It will be more useful if you make the anchor something that you can 'fire' discretely next time you need it. For example, touching your face in a certain place or clenching your fist.

Use the anchor each day for a week, each time noticing more internally, externally, narrow and broad.

Plan an hour somewhere where you won't be interrupted.

Then 'fire' your anchor as you recap what you did at the end of modules 1 - 5.

how to be exceptional

awareness
awareness of others

Module 7 : Awareness of others

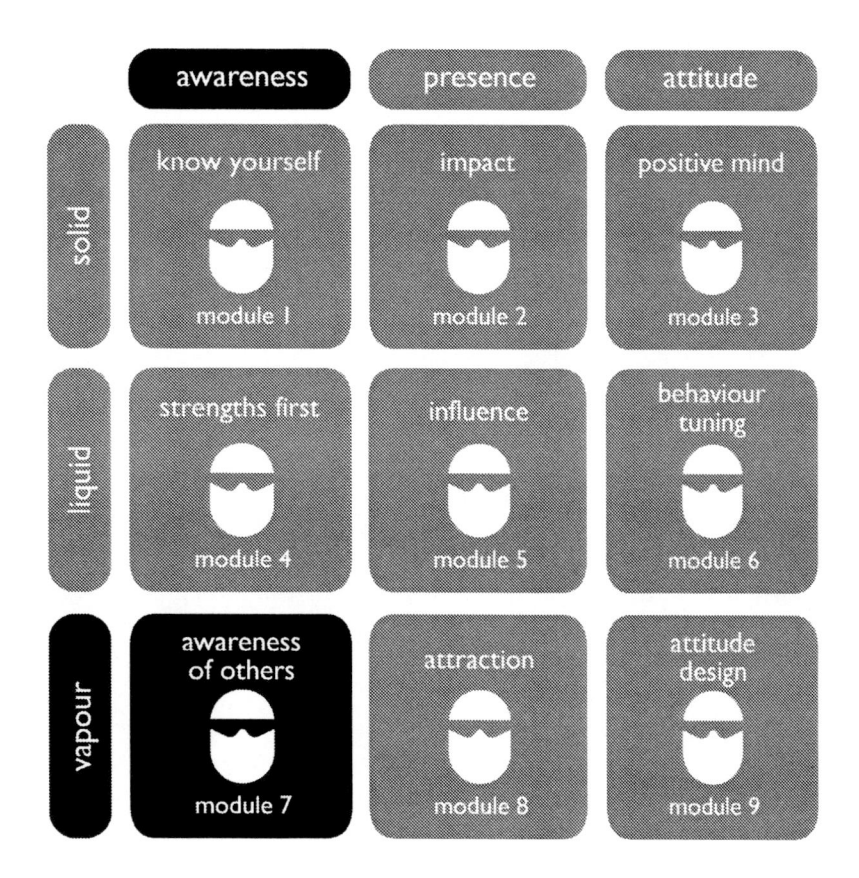

	awareness	presence	attitude
solid	know yourself module 1	impact module 2	positive mind module 3
liquid	strengths first module 4	influence module 5	behaviour tuning module 6
vapour	**awareness of others module 7**	attraction module 8	attitude design module 9

In the first two thirds of this programme, you should have been introspective; noticing things about yourself so that you can become more exceptional.

But it's generally others who judge whether you're truly exceptional.

In module 7, we consider how exceptional people interact with the people around them. These models make you more exceptional and allow others realise that you are.

Motives

People don't do things for no reason. Whether their actions are perceived as good or bad, there is always some intent behind their action. A useful **map of reality** is that people generally have a positive intent behind their actions. So, I'd like you to consider a **principle** that simplifies peoples' behaviour into three base motives.

People are motivated by **achievement** and want to get things done, gaining recognition or personal pride from doing them.

People are motivated by **relationships** and want to interact with others and maintain strong personal bonds with them.

People are motivated by **control** and want to have an involvement in how things are done and ensure that they're done in the right way.

Deep down, whenever somebody does something, it's to satisfy one of these base motives. When we looked at **tribal archetypes** in module 4, we considered **what** people do best and **what** their natural strength is.

Motives differ in that they consider **why** people do specific things. It helps you improve your awareness and make more sense of the actions and words of other people.

When you begin to better understand what motivates people, you can use this information to **reframe** the way that you communicate so that it has a greater appeal to their motives.

awareness
awareness of others

I want to make it clear within this generalisation of complex behaviour that people cannot merely be tagged with one of these three labels. For sure, individuals will be biased towards a certain base motive but I'd like you to consider that what motivates people also has to be taken in **context** with what it is they're doing. For example, buying a CD may have a different base motive for the same person as deciding how to plan their pension.

In a given task, three people could have completely different personal needs and motives:

Achievement
'I want to ensure that we do the job on time.'

Relationships
'I want to know that everybody is happy with what they have to do.'

Control
'I want to be confident that we are on track and will deliver on time.'

Listen for cues that tell you how others are motivated.

People who are motivated by **achievement** like:

- results
- outcomes
- tangible things
- facts & figures
- status & kudos
- comparisons & benchmarks

People who are motivated by **relationships** like:

- discussion
- debate
- interaction
- harmony
- events
- communication

People who are motivated by **control** like:

- plans
- status of progress
- governance
- prioritisation
- metrics
- processes
- quality
- consistency

Asking simple questions like 'What's important to you about this?' or 'Talk to me about your thoughts on this…' are great ways of eliciting an individual's motives on a subject.

> Think of something that's important to you right now.
>
> What is it about this thing that makes it so important to you? Which of the three base motives is driving it for you?
>
> If you were motivated by one of the other base motives, how might that change it? Does it get more or less important? Can you adjust this thing so that it also considers one or both of the other base motives?

When you set direction for others, ensure that your communication addresses all three base motives. That way, you're more likely to motivate more people.

Use the motives model to check whether your own decisions and actions can be improved or communicated in a way that has a greater appeal to people who are motivated by different things to you.

Consider your actions and words as a complex ecology. You need to use each component in perfect balance in order to ensure that everybody gets just enough of what they each need to survive.

awareness
awareness of others

When you make decisions or set direction, go into **bullet time** and notice which of the three base motives you are most influenced by. You'll notice that the language you use naturally is biased towards your primary motive.

So press **pause** and rotate around from each perspective, asking yourself what you'd do or say differently from the other two motives.

Add your new awareness of the other motives to your decision or message and then press **play** again. The ecologically balanced broadcast will considers all three motives and will enable you to fine tune your actions and words.

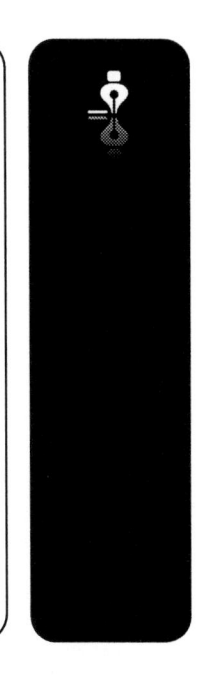

People are their emotions

In order to make sense of other people, you must first make sense of the things that they outwardly express that inform you of their **state**. These things are their **emotions**.

The literal translation of **emotion** from its two Latin source words is **outward movement** (ex / motio). This evokes the notion of gestures and physical expressions.

> "People are their emotions. To understand who a person is, it is necessary to understand emotion."
>
> **Norman Denzin**

If you can sense a person's **state**, you can have greater empathy with them. Once you have empathy, you can communicate with them in a way that is appropriate to their **state**.

If you accept that people are their emotions and take Denzin's quote literally, you can begin to **see through** the **individuals** that you're communicating with and **focus on their emotions**. In essence, all you need to do if you want to communicate with people is **alter their state**. If you focus on their state, you're working with their emotions.

When you communicate with an outcome of affecting a person's **emotions**, you are able to change their **state**. If you can change a person's state without breaking **rapport**, you can **influence** very elegantly.

If you do happen to break **rapport** by changing somebody's emotional **state**, you can still **influence** them.

awareness
awareness of others

> Sometimes, it is crucial to change a person's **state** if you are to make an impact with your communication.
>
> Imagine trying to warn somebody of a severe risk when their state is one of glee.
>
> Consider trying to motivate somebody to do a great job when their state is worry.

Emotions require **context**. Being impatient can be negative in a certain context, such as waiting in a traffic jam, or it can be positive in others, like wanting to finish a puzzle.

If you were to not take yourself too seriously, amusement may be a positive emotion. It may also be a negative emotion during a serious situation.

The list of emotions below has been ranked based on my **map of reality** as to whether each **emotion** is positive, negative or neutral in the **context** of becoming exceptional.

emotion	-	=	+	meaning
Acceptance	✓			
Agitation	✓			
Alarm		✓		
Amusement		✓		
Anger	✓			
Angst	✓			
Anticipation		✓		
Apprehension		✓		
Apathy	✓			
Awe		✓		
Bitterness	✓			
Boredom	✓			
Calmness			✓	
Comfort			✓	
Contentment			✓	
Confidence			✓	

how to be exceptional

emotion	-	=	+	meaning
Courage			✓	
Depression	✓			
Disappointment		✓		
Discontentment	✓			
Disgust	✓			
Desire			✓	
Delight			✓	
Elation			✓	
Euphoria			✓	
Embarrassment	✓			
Ennui	✓			a feeling of weariness and dissatisfaction
Envy	✓			
Ecstasy			✓	
Fear	✓			
Friendship			✓	
Frustration	✓			
Glee			✓	
Gladness			✓	
Gratitude		✓		
Grief	✓			
Guilt	✓			
Hate	✓			
Happiness			✓	
Homesickness		✓		
Honour			✓	
Hope			✓	
Horror	✓			
Humility			✓	
Joy			✓	
Jealousy	✓			
Kindness			✓	
Loneliness	✓			
Love			✓	
Lust			✓	
Limerence	✓			intrusive thinking about something and a longing for reciprocation
Modesty			✓	
Nervousness		✓		

awareness
awareness of others

emotion	-	=	+	meaning
Negativity	✓			
Nostalgia		✓		
Pain	✓			
Patience			✓	
Peace			✓	
Phobia	✓			
Pity			✓	
Pride			✓	
Rage	✓			
Remorse			✓	
Sadness	✓			
Schadenfreude	✓			pleasure taken from someone else's misfortune
Self-pity	✓			
Shame	✓			
Shyness	✓			
Sorrow	✓			
Shock		✓		
Suffering	✓			
Surprise		✓		
Suspense		✓		
Terror	✓			
Unhappiness	✓			
Vulnerability	✓			
Worry	✓			

You can use this list to design ways to get people in and out of **states** or to move people from one state to another.

Because you've already experienced a wide range of emotions, you can imagine how a person may look or behave during certain emotions. Once you interpret other peoples' emotions, you can **pace and lead** them to different emotional states by altering your behaviour. As you do this, they will follow your lead and change their own emotional state.

For example, to move somebody from **anger** towards **calmness**, you could pace and lead them by becoming calmer yourself. As you do this, they will calm down too. Shouting back at an angry person only serves to make them even angrier. Slowing down your breathing rate, talking in slow, soft tones and blinking more slowly will gradually calm them down.

To move somebody, or even a group of people, from **apathy** towards **modesty**, tell them how good they are at the things they do when they bother to care enough about them.

> "When dealing with people, remember you are not dealing with creatures of logic, but creatures of emotion."
>
> **Dale Carnegie**

To move people from **envy** towards **awe**, make whatever they are envious of even more impressive and desirable.

To move somebody from **fear** to **hope**, listen to them and then offer guidance and assistance.

The most important aspect of changing the emotions of others is being **congruent**. You can't make people feel happy if your face says that you're unhappy. You can't make people feel euphoric if your voice tone says you're worried. You can't get people to be patient if you are tapping your fingers in a frustrated way.

It is possible to **look through an individual** and **communicate more directly with their emotions**.

It isn't just **your** emotions in the **TEA model** that you can change with your own actions. You can do things that **sway others into different emotional states**.

Pace and **lead** and remain **congruent**; as you adopt certain emotions, others will follow you into a similar state.

awareness
awareness of others

Sounds, pictures and feelings

When people think, they use different internal strategies to structure their thoughts. Some think in pictures, some think in sounds and others think using feelings.

Although people use all of these modes of thinking from time to time, most people have a preference for one way of thinking.

Their preferred way of representing their thoughts will become evident in the language that they use.

These three strategies of thinking are important because they describe how individuals express their **maps of reality**. Two people may have the same concept in mind but express it in totally different ways.

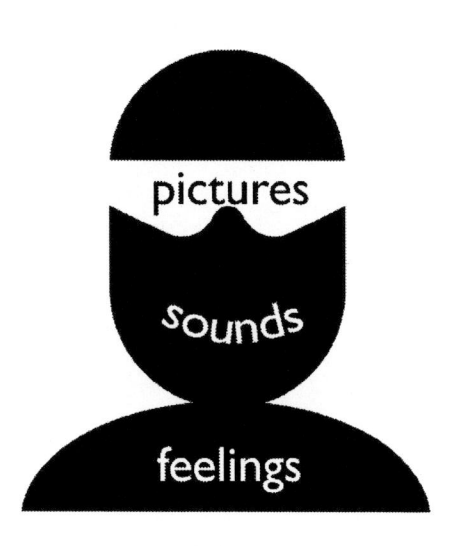

> You may already **see** what I mean, **hear** what I'm saying or have a **grasp** of this. If you don't, let me paint you a **picture** and offer you my **story** so that it **hits** home more fully.

A large proportion of misunderstanding and even failure to understand at all can be put down to the fact that the parties involved are using language that doesn't match. For example, a person uses picture based language to explain something to a person who prefers language that uses sounds.

Using language that is heavily biased towards one way of thinking can **unconsciously** break **rapport** with those who have different preferences.

This is a complex topic that we'll build on in module 8. For now, I want to make you aware of the following:

You'll have a preferred way of thinking that will differ from a proportion of the people you interact with. The largest proportion of people prefer to think using **pictures**. This is followed by those with a preference for thinking in **sounds**. Far fewer people prefer to think using **feelings**.

You'll unconsciously **use language that is meaningful** to your own way of thinking but which won't be as meaningful to everyone you interact with.

Fortunately, there are ways of overcoming this. One method is to use neutral words that don't have a bias towards one of the strategies:

biased language	neutral language
o **picture** a place	o **imagine** being in a place
o I **told** you that you were good	o **think** of a time when you did something good
o It just **feels** wrong	o You **know** when it's wrong

Conversational business dialogue tends not to have a specific bias. Although this makes it good for people to be able to understand, it's very difficult for people to get excited about because it doesn't appeal to any preferred thinking strategy.

Instead, you could **cycle** through the different ways of representing thoughts, ensuring that you **highlight** words that **resonate** with each strategy in **turn**. Although this **sounds** quite **hard**, it is actually much easier to **grasp** than **fiddling** with **dull**, neutral words.

awareness
awareness of others

Sprinkling your day-to-day communication with carefully chosen words that have a very strong bias towards each way of thinking will make it more appealing to people with those preferred strategies.

I always read through my e-mails before pressing send and check for a specific bias of words. I am a very visual person, using **imagery** and **graphical** language to **illustrate** my **views**.

So I review my words to find ones that **sound** better and create a certain **resonance** when I **compose** my overall **message**.

I also **feel** that it's important to ensure that the **structure** of my message is **solid** and that it **flows** between sections **smoothly**.

Begin to notice your preferred way of thinking. **Tune your words** so that they appeal to other people who may think in a different way to you.

Use bright **pictures**, rich **sounds** and strong **feelings**

When you describe things, **paint vivid visions** and make sure you make all the right **noises** so that people **hear** your key messages.

As you explain yourself, get people into the same **groove** as you so that they come along for the **ride**.

Filters on reality

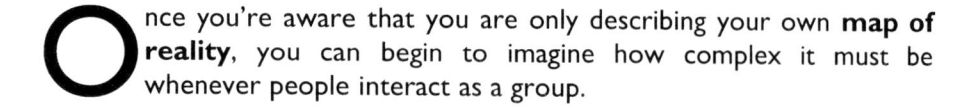

Once you're aware that you are only describing your own **map of reality**, you can begin to imagine how complex it must be whenever people interact as a group.

Each person has their own unique **map of reality** which either overlaps with of varies from the next person's map. It's as if each person is looking at the World through a set of polarized sunglasses and sees the same thing in a slightly different way.

There are times in group situations where much debate and discussion takes place but no agreement is made. It's as if certain people not only have the wrong end of the stick, but actually have different sticks.

This is often because nobody has taken time to **align** peoples' **filters on reality**. Each person uses the same term but interprets it to mean a slightly different thing based on their unique personal experience.

In module 1, we either **saw**, **discussed** or **covered** how your own **map of reality** can be used to ensure that you don't break **rapport** with others by couching your opinions as opinions and not as facts.

If people feel very strongly about something, they describe it using words that evoke and support their **filter on reality**. They may say something like 'this is a **massive** issue for me' or 'this will have a **huge** impact'.

The **extent** of the words that people use to describe things is a good indication of their **filter on reality** of a situation.

awareness
awareness of others

Choose a subject that describes the **extent** of something - **size** is a great example.

Imagine a line with a word in the middle that describes the average middle point of size, for example **medium**.

Plot other size words like **big, small, huge, tiny** along the line representing their **extent**. Mark words with a small extent to the left and a larger extent to the right. Stop when you can't think of any more relevant words.

Now, ask somebody else to do the same thing on a new line as you feed them with the same words.

Your individual **maps of reality** will differ greatly from each other and words that describe something as simple as size will have different meanings to you both.

Is **huge** bigger or smaller than **massive**?

To get a group of people to be exceptional, it is important that you align their **filters on reality** as far as possible. Act as an interpreter to their **maps of the reality** and smooth out any misunderstandings.

Not only will the group become more exceptional, but you will be considered to be an exceptional 'interpreter'.

- Take time to agree and clarify terminology

- Chunk people down to **specifics** when they are too vague

- Chunk up to **principles** so that people can make assumptions about unnecessary detail

how to be exceptional

- Clarify generalisations such as they, he, it, always, never

- Demonstrate to people how something might **look** different from another perspective by **putting** them in another person's shoes

- Use **contextual healing** to enable people who are not up to speed to accelerate their understanding

---

Act as an interpreter and ensure that people have hold of the **same stick** before they try to grab the right end of it.

When you **align** peoples' **filters on reality** the combined **light**, **sound** or **fluid** can pass through efficiently and concentrate properly.

awareness
awareness of others

Perception

Perception is based on position. That is to **say**, the perception that you have depends on where you are **standing** and you'll **see** things differently from varying positions.

Because you are yourself and not somebody else, you experience the majority of things through your own **map of reality**. Your **values** and **specific** experience therefore give you a certain **perception** of situations. As you interact with people, they are unlikely to be aware of your perception just as you are unlikely to be aware of theirs.

Perception isn't vastly different from your **map of reality**. But there's a distinction that I'd like you to make - **you can alter your perception in real time as you interact with people**.

Just as your **map of reality** is based on the **values** that you've accumulated throughout your life, your **perception** is based on your position at a given point in time and in a certain **context**.

When you interact with another person, there are three positions of perception that you could take:

- o   your own position
- o   their position
- o   an observer's position

> "Before you criticize someone, walk a mile in his shoes. That way, when you criticize him, you will be a mile away, and you will have his shoes."
>
> **Chuck Humphrey**

If you can manage to step into these different positions, you will become aware of things that are happening that are restricting you from being truly exceptional.

During certain interactions, go into **bullet time** and use the following process:

1. From your own position, notice what you **see**, **hear** and **feel**.

2. Step into the position of the person you're interacting with. **Notice** the **things about you** that they will be noticing now; your expressions, voice tone, words, posture and mannerisms.

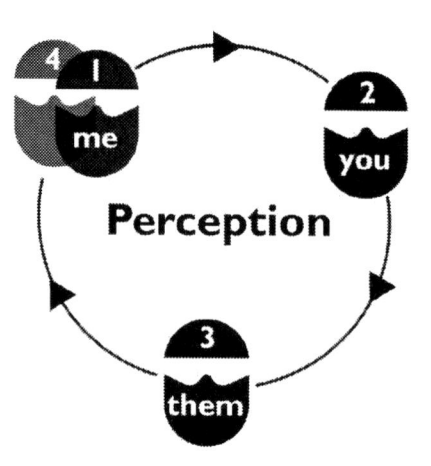

3. Next, step into the position of an observer and notice the way that both of you are interacting. How are you both positioned? Who's **transmitting** and who's **receiving**? What is your level of **rapport?**

4. Finally, step back into your own position and **adjust what you're doing** based on what you've observed.

This process gives you empathy and insight. You observe yourself in ways that you wouldn't usually consider and you become more aware of tiny things about your behaviour that others notice all of the time.

You can use different perceptual positions to heighten your awareness and adjust your perception as you interact with people around you.

This offers you a **real time feedback** mechanism that you can use to judge how your **actions** are affecting the **thoughts** and **emotions** of others.

Doing this will give you greater empathy and improved **rapport**.

awareness
awareness of others

Module 7 - Exercise

Find three examples of written material from books, newspapers, magazines or web pages, making sure that you can write on them.

Using three different colours, circle or highlight the words that respectively evoke **pictures**, **sounds** and **feelings.**

Then, re-read the material, identifying the words that indicate the **extent** of the author's **filter on reality**.

Choose an example statement and identify how you would align the author's map of reality with your own.

how to be exceptional

presence
attraction

Module 8 : Attraction

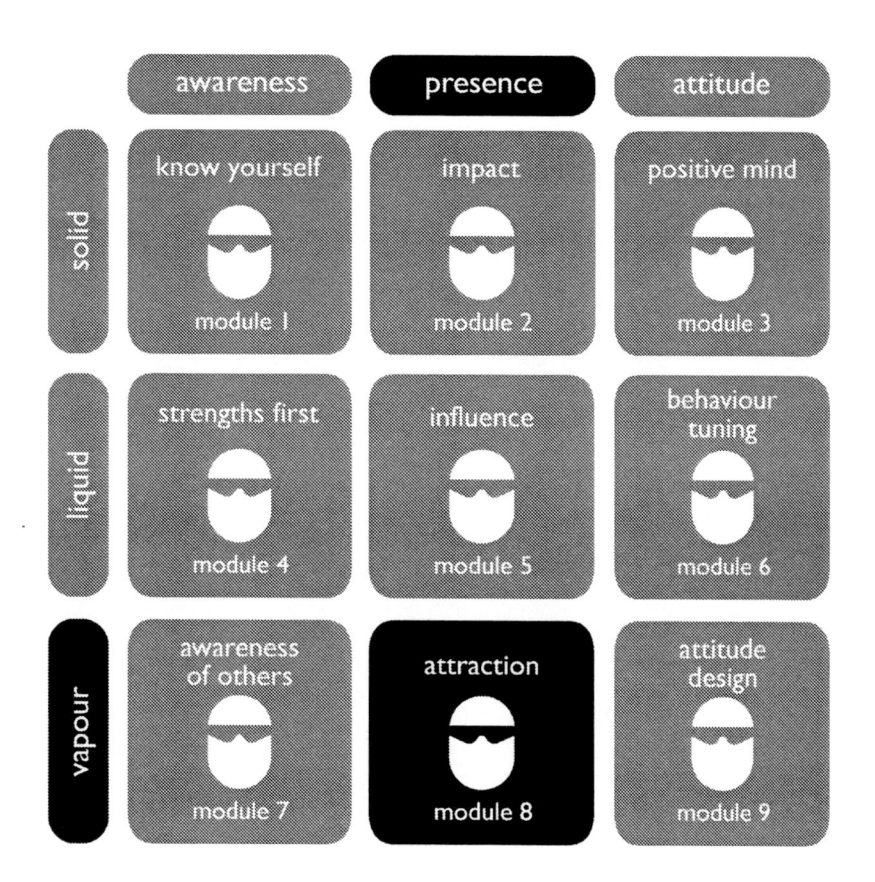

	awareness	presence	attitude
solid	know yourself — module 1	impact — module 2	positive mind — module 3
liquid	strengths first — module 4	influence — module 5	behaviour tuning — module 6
vapour	awareness of others — module 7	**attraction — module 8**	attitude design — module 9

Appearance alone cannot attract people. Being attractive is about the way that you choose to communicate. Attraction is about getting other people to want to be with you and do things with you.

Module 8 introduces a number of models that enable you to attract people effectively and elegantly. Having people around you who want to be around you and who truly believe in you is crucial to being exceptional.

how to be exceptional

How are you today?

Whenever you meet somebody, there's a really simple experiment that you can try out as part of your introduction. Just ask how they are today and notice their response.

I'm sure you've either witnessed or been involved in an exchange along the followings lines:

Person 1:   'How are you?'

Person 2:   'Not too bad - you?'

Person 1:   'I'm not too bad either.'

There are two interesting things that I'd like you to notice about this:

1. Person 1 usually responds in an almost identical way to Person 2. This is an unconscious **pace** and **lead**.

2. How Person 2 'is' starts with **bad** as a benchmark and measures how far away they are from it; **not too** bad.

This is a true **glass half empty** in contrast to **glass half full** attitude.

Although you occasionally hear a person using slightly less negative language such as 'fine' or 'OK', it's unusual that you have somebody respond with positive language such as 'I'm very well thanks' or 'I'm great'.

presence
attraction

I went to a very exclusive Italian restaurant recently and, as the waiter was seating us, I asked him how he was.

His response, said in an Italian accent:

"Just a little bit better than fantastic."

He didn't ask how we were, but if he had, I'd have said I felt fantastic too.

When you are asked how you are, if you respond with a positive **state** and do it **congruently**, it gets a totally different response from people.

- If they really do feel positive, you get a positive response back from them because you **pace** and **lead** them.

- If they are feeling negative, you get a response along the lines of 'what are you so happy about?'

The way you respond when somebody asks you how you are is a great opportunity to go in to **bullet time** and reinforce **your own state** so that you stop them in their tracks and **alter their state**.

Hypnotists use a technique called **pattern interruption** to put people into an **altered state** of consciousness.

Pattern interruption involves identifying a process that usually happens automatically, like saying 'not too bad' when being asked how you are, or shaking somebody's hand, and then breaking that process. A handshake for example is **an unconscious action** and **has no** real **beginning, middle** and **end**; it just kind of happens.

What hypnotists know is this; if you **give a process** like this **a middle** when it doesn't usually have one, you **create a mild state of confusion** in people. It's then possible to utilise their state to make suggestions.

At this point, whatever you tell them goes straight in at an **unconscious** level and makes a big **impact** on them.

It's as if they lower any barriers they have and just say:

'OK, tell me whatever you want to now, I'm listening...'

Here's how a pattern interruption might work as part of an introduction conversation:

Person 1: 'How are you?'

Person 2: 'Do you know, I feel absolutely fantastic today.'

Person 1: 'Really....? Why's that?'

> **OK, tell me whatever you want to now, I'm listening...**

Person 2: 'Well ... I just **feel** like we're going to have a really good session today because we're all so **fired** up for it.'

presence
attraction

If you want to improve your presence, you need to attract people and change their **state**. Use your introduction and small talk as a **pattern interruption** to get others in to the right state.

Here are a couple of 'How are you today?' responses that will create a positive state:

- Bordering on spectacular
- Absolutely fantastic
- Possibly unstoppable
- Pretty much on fire
- **VERY** good
- On top of the World
- Raring to go
- Brimming with energy

Being interesting

Nobody likes a bore. So you'd think that most people would spend a great deal of time becoming more and more interesting. In my experience, you don't. Instead, you accept who you are and shy away from making yourself really interesting to the people around you. I have a theory that because people spend so much time inside their own minds, they actually get bored of themselves and stop being interesting.

My advice is to treat every interaction as an opportunity to make yourself interesting to the people that you're with. Treat every conversation as a first date and make sure that the people you're trying to make an **impact** on, **influence** or **attract** want to spend even more time in your company.

Have you ever been in an environment where people have had to introduce themselves and the person running things has said something like **'Tell me your name, where you're from and something interesting about you'**?

You can see the terror on the faces of certain people as they think to themselves **'but I'm not interesting'**.

Some people even introduce themselves **'I'm Dave from Derbyshire and there isn't really anything interesting about me.'**

Or, worse still **'...the only interesting thing about me is that I can't think of anything interesting to say!'**

presence
attraction

If you spend your spare time watching EastEnders, you'll end up just like the characters; they'll probably **pace** and **lead** you. **Stop it**. Start to become more interesting. Do things that make you more interesting immediately.

Make the things that you do sound more interesting. If you don't have anything interesting to say about now, say something interesting about what you want to do in the future.

> "There is no such thing on earth as an uninteresting subject; the only thing that can exist is an uninterested person."
>
> **G.K. Chesterton**

Here are a few interesting things about me off the top of my head...

- A friend and I own a 1970s VW camper that we're restoring
- I've made 2 guinea pig runs in the last 3 months
- I run an online store for my local rugby club
- I never throw out my old notepads - I have over 50 of them
- I've got more shoes than my wife
- I can't see new technology without wanting to play with it
- I'm writing a book of metaphors to promote good children's behaviour
- My wife and I run an entertainment business in our spare time
- I have a chicken suit but I've not worn it outside the house yet
- I've been on a BBC Radio 4 comedy show
- I've had a blood transfusion
- My friends and I have a stag weekend in Europe every year even through we're all married

how to be exceptional

Interesting things don't have to be about you. They can be facts that you collect or learn - unusual stories, bizarre statistics, trivia and oddities. Even nonsense questions that stir interest. I somehow managed to get on BBC Radio 4 by asking my friends what the opposite of a knife was.

- Did you know that umami is actually a taste just like bitter, sour or sweet?
- The word gnome comes from the Greek *gnosis* meaning knowledge
- Thomas Edison left 3,000 notepads containing his ideas and experiments when he died
- Rotavator is the longest palindrome in the English language; it reads the same either way
- There is a game called Triolet which is Scrabble with numbers – how easy must that be?
- The only antonym of antonym is opposite but synonym doesn't have an antonym

When you're interesting, you command attention and attract people more easily. When you attract people, you gain **presence**.

Go and find ways to make yourself more interesting. If you're already interesting, make yourself even more interesting. Being interesting is one of the key attributes that attracts people to you.

Make yourself interesting and make it your business to find more interesting things. Read diversely, speak to strangers. Ask people questions about the things that interest them. Get a hobby. Go to unusual places. Visit random websites. Read Wikipedia. Research subjects for no reason. Make lists. Become fact hungry. **Become interesting.**

presence
attraction

Totems and cults

Five thousand years ago, geographically dispersed people in Asia, Europe, Africa, Australia and the Arctic were using totems. They adopted natural and supernatural objects as focal points for their energy and worship. Their chosen **totem** objects were metaphors for the beliefs and traits that they decided to live by within their early civilizations.

Many cultures chose animals such as eagles, wolves or bears as their totem; a trend adopted by modern day sports teams in American Football, Basketball, Ice Hockey and Rugby. Others chose less animate objects such as plants, stones or precious materials.

The totem became something that people would gather around for understanding and insight.

Alternatively, it was something they would wear or carry to give them strength and willpower.

You can **create totems** in whatever you do:

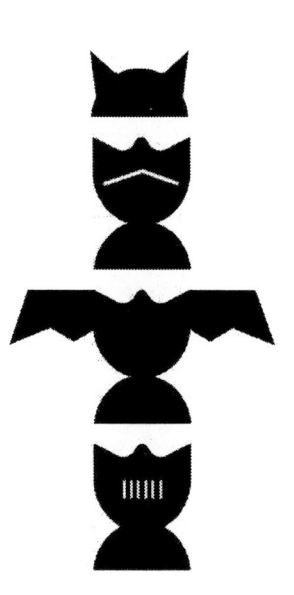

Create a diagram that explains how you want people to perform. Establish a metaphor for how you want them to behave at a certain time, such as a project or team name. Laminate a list of **principles** as a handy, constant reminder of how you intend to do what you do.

I believe that you can **attract** people with the **totems** that you create.

People are attracted much more **towards** totems than they are by traditional, mundane documents such as the memos, agendas, processes and procedures that unexceptional people tend to use. Totems inspire and motivate people, giving them hope and direction.

how to be exceptional

> Which is the more attractive, a **project initiation document** documenting the phases of a project or an **image of a snow capped mountain** with base-camps on the ascent indicating each leg of the climb?
>
> o   Which is more memorable?
> o   Which evokes a greater sense of achievement?
> o   Which makes you feel like you want to take part in the challenge?
> o   Which one is most likely to be drawn, impromptu, on a flipchart to explain where you're at?

A totem is a simple, iconic, engaging, meaningful object that conveys your vision, direction, **values** or **purpose** in a concise memorable way.

When you want to **attract** people to go with you in a certain direction, build a rich and powerful totem. Build it using **pictures**, **sounds** and **feelings** and make it central to your actions. Once you've built it, reference it at every opportunity.

Now you have your totem, gather people around it. **Cults** are select groups of people who become devoted to the beliefs of a group.

The word has gathered negative connotations in recent years due to some unfortunate happenings with religious sects and fundamentalism. However, in both history and reality, cults are much more neutral than the media bias would have us believe.

Once you get past the religious definitions of a cult, you'll find more balanced definitions along the lines of a '**great devotion to a person, idea, object, movement, or work.**'

Getting others to adopt this kind of attitude is true **attraction**.

presence
attraction

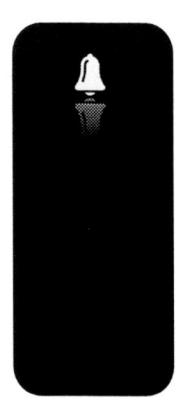

> In the book **Built to Last**, following a great deal of research, James Collins and Jerry Porras, defined '**cult-like cultures**' as one of the key attributes of visionary organisations.
>
> In the **The 48 Laws of Power**, a study of great and powerful leaders throughout history, Robert Greene and Joost Elffers assert Law 27 as '**Play on people's "need to believe" to create a cult like following**'

Once you have a strong totem, you can establish a **cult-like culture**. I'm not suggesting mind control, brainwashing, religious sects and the like.

What I am suggesting is that you identify a **select of group of people who fully believe in your totem**, but who don't treat you as a cult leader. That's a key distinction; they believe in your ideology more than they believe in you as a person.

> Why does Disney call a work shift at Disneyland a 'Performance'?
>
> It's done to create a sense of belonging, to encourage social interaction between members and to create behaviour **congruent** with their **totem**.

Your group must become 100% bought in to where you want to go and **intolerant** of people who aren't; either **buy-in or get out**. They must become evangelists for what you want to achieve without seeming elitist. Your totem will elegantly help you achieve this.

> If you're taking people on a journey and want to **attract** them to go with you, build a **totem**. Then create a close-knit, **cult-like** tribe around it who are intrinsically connected to it.

Submodalities

We discussed the different ways that people think using **pictures**, **sounds** and **feelings** in module 7. When you speak to other people using these three ways of communicating, you can use special words to intensify or soften the emotions that they have. These extra words are **submodalities.**

If I were to paint a **picture** for you of your future, it may evoke a certain **emotion**. But I could make the emotion attached to it even greater using visual submodalities to describe the picture part.

So, let me take a **crisp white canvas** and **paint** you a **vivid colourful picture** of your **bright** future.

If you like the **sound** of this, you'll probably like it even more if I turn up the **volume** and switch on the **surround sound** so that you can get a **crystal clear** sense of what I'm **saying** to you.

It **feels** much better when you add in these extra words. It's as if they actually **touch** you somewhere and **push** a **pulse** along your **spine** producing a **jolt** of extra reality **inside** your mind.

Submodalities are **extra words** that evoke **extra emotions**; they change the intensity of your senses. If you use them, you'll **attract** people more because you'll be making their **state** and **emotions** even **stronger**.

How interested would you be in spending more time with somebody who makes you feel even better than you already do?

presence
attraction

If you choose to, you can use submodalities for the opposite purpose too.

It's possible to break **rapport** very easily by **painting dark pictures** of a person's future, giving them a **sharp jab** that they don't want so that they reflect **quietly** on what might happen to them.

Use **submodalities** in your language to amplify **emotions** and **states**. They are **extra words** that evoke **extra emotions**.

For **pictures**, play with:

- brightness
- colour
- contrast
- dimension - flat vs. 3D
- borders and frames
- speed of movement
- focus
- lights
- shadows

For **sounds**, play with:

- volume
- bass
- treble
- depth
- direction
- tone
- resonance
- clarity
- harmony

For **feelings**, play with:

- texture
- temperature
- weight
- balance
- intensity
- impact
- internal sensations
- harsh vs. gentle
- wind and water

how to be exceptional

Rich language

Good words are attractive. I believe that if you say the same words as everybody around you, your ability to attract will be similar to theirs. Ultimately, you'll attract the same people to the same extent.

If you use **rich language**, you'll create greater **attraction** and attract different people to a different extent.

Invest time in defining a unique and interesting style of rich language; certain words that become your trademarks and single you out as being different to the crowd who use dull language and clichés.

The following techniques equip you with ways to add richness to your language so that people listen more intently and want to listen to you more often.

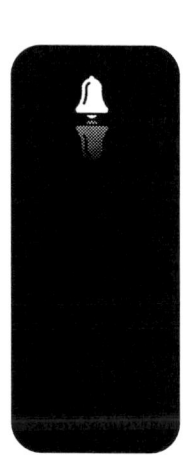

There are **unusual** or **old fashioned** words that stand out in modern dialogue:

Instead of	Try
Assume I'm right for a minute…	If you **entertain** the **notion** that this is correct…
We need to tell them what we think…	I'd expect us to be **quite vociferous**…

presence
attraction

> There are specialised words that can be **borrowed** from other **industries** such as medicine or engineering:
>
> | **Instead of** | **Try** |
> |---|---|
> | We need to look at eight different parts of this… | There are eight **splines** for us to **inspect**… |
> | The problems are likely to continue… | We have a number of **chronic** problems… |

> There are certain times when people use words that are **almost out of context** but still make sense:
>
> | **Instead of** | **Try** |
> |---|---|
> | There were a lot of mistakes… | There was a **cacophony** of mistakes… |
> | He only turns up when he feels like it… | His attendance is **undulant**… |

> There are **foreign** words that can be inserted into English so that they immediately jump out:
>
> | **Instead of** | **Try** |
> |---|---|
> | We need to start again from scratch… | We need **carte blanche** to do what's required of us… |
> | You should try your best and more… | Perform **ad astra**… |

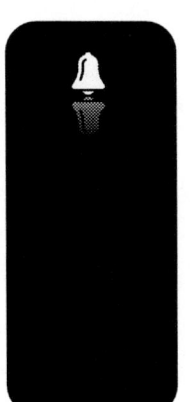

how to be exceptional

> There are **metaphoric** phrases that describe a situation in a nutshell. These are useful because they also alter peoples' frame of reference and **reframe context**. Just watch out for clichés:
>
> | Instead of | Try |
> | --- | --- |
> | Because you've noticed an increase in costs doesn't mean that we're making a loss… | **A dog has four legs.** The fact an animal has four legs doesn't make it a dog… |
> | It's impossible to do all of this work at once… | It would make more sense not trying to **boil the ocean**… |

When you use language in this way, you create **attraction** that may materialise in any number of ways. People may:

- ask you there and then what a word or phrase means
- go away and look it up, finding you curious
- talk about you afterwards
- absorb the word or phase unconsciously and begin using it themselves; a true sign of **rapport**
- ask for more information about a concept relating to a word you used; 'I didn't know you were an engineer…'

I can't predict what will happen **specifically** because I don't yet know which words you will choose and the **context** in which you'll use them.

But I do know that when you do use different words like these, you'll cause people to pay more attention to you and create a minor **pattern interrupt** that makes them say:

presence
attraction

'OK, tell me whatever you want to now, I'm listening...'

Find rich words that work for you and use them. Use them gradually and casually and you will create **attraction**.

- Don't **be too clever**
- Don't **use words that you don't understand**
- Don't **overcook it**
- But please, do **be different**

how to be exceptional

Module 8 - Exercise

Find the work you did at the end of module 4; your revised **who I am** statement and **values**. Begin to apply some **attraction** models.

- make it more **interesting**
- add **submodalities**
- use **rich language**

When you've finished, prepare a **how are you today?** response ready to use on the next person who asks.

When you use it, notice the reaction you get.

attitude
attitude design

Module 9 : Attitude design

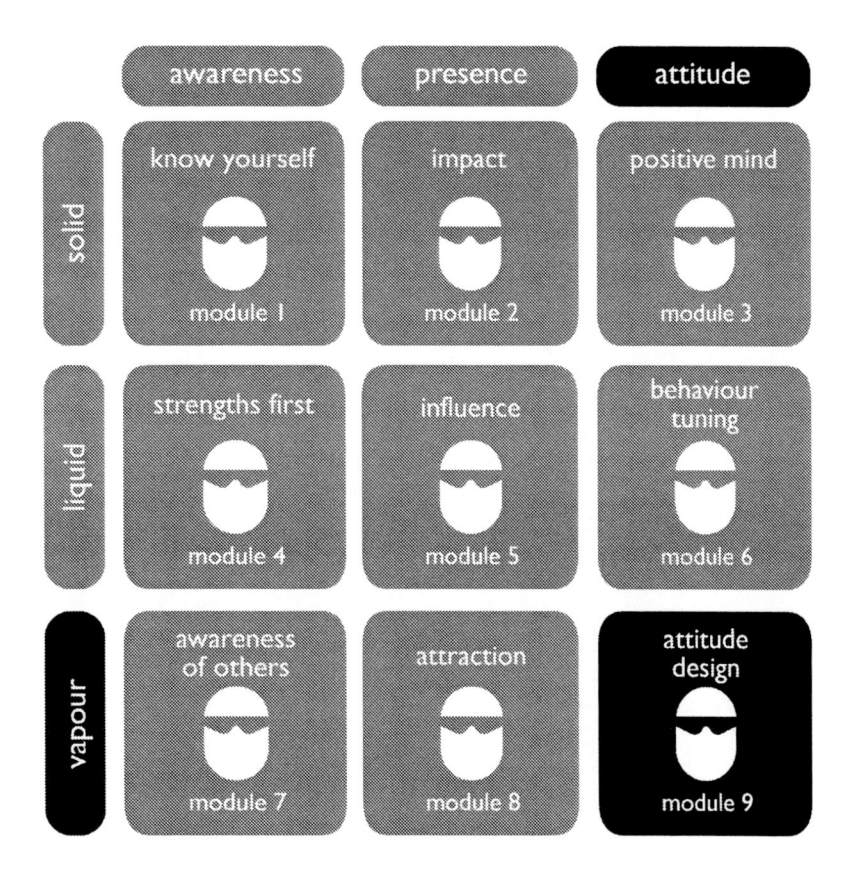

	awareness	presence	attitude
solid	know yourself module 1	impact module 2	positive mind module 3
liquid	strengths first module 4	influence module 5	behaviour tuning module 6
vapour	awareness of others module 7	attraction module 8	**attitude design module 9**

You've made it to the end of the beginning. In module 9 you will find models that help you to define and redefine yourself.

You will also realise why your **who I am** statement and **values** are so important to being exceptional and continually becoming more and more exceptional at the things you do.

Be an expert or authority

If you want to be exceptional at whatever you do, you first need to be credible. If you want to be perceived as credible, you **congruently** need to behave credibly.

The simplest way of **unconsciously** letting people know that you are both exceptional and credible is to become an expert or authority on something.

There's a point that you hit in your life where you realise that you can use the term **'in my experience…'** before you make statements.

It was a complete surprise to me the first time I realised I'd said 'in my experience' out loud. I was around 25 and I'd only been working for three years but it felt right to say what I'd said. It felt right because I'd been involved in something every day for three years and I believed that I truly had expertise in that area - more so than anybody else I'd met.

It was odd because whenever I prefixed my statements or even opinions with 'in my experience…' people listened; colleagues, customers and suppliers all took notice. It occurred to me that the only person telling these people that I was an expert was **me.**

I'm not suggesting that proclaiming or pretending that you're an expert is all you need to do. I'm telling you to actually **become an expert**. Identify what it is **specifically** that you do best. Then take time to research, understand, articulate, discuss and conclude what it is that you know. Finally, make sure that people know that that's what you know.

attitude
attitude design

If you want to be perceived as an expert or authority, in order to be convincing, you need to consider a number of things:

1. **Context** – you can be an expert in something at some level. Just make sure that you set the right level. I'd be lying if I were to say that I'm a World renowned e-commerce expert. But in the circles that I move, I know as much as anybody I know. That makes me an authority in that **context**.

2. **Permission** – don't wait for somebody to come and give you a badge that says 'expert in property investment'. Once you're comfortable that you know enough, make your own badge.

3. **Perspective** – have a perspective. Make sure that you have opinions on your subject that stand out. This could be as simple as:

    o your own way of describing something

    o a **totem** that you use to explain your **bold** views

    o combining a number of things together – 'I apply interior design techniques to the way that I write marketing copy'

    o distilling your own perspective from other peoples' views

4. **Identity** – consciously adopt an identity so that you become more credible. We'll discuss this in more detail in **attitude design**.

> There is a certain subtlety to the way you tell people that you're an expert or authority. Just saying that you're an expert isn't the most tactful approach. Do it so that it just blends in with everyday conversations:
>
> o I specialise in…
>
> o When I did my research on this, I concluded that…
>
> o What we've found when we've worked with customers in this area is…
>
> o I'm often asked what my views are on this and I generally say…

how to be exceptional

When you want to describe yourself as an **expert** or **authority**, there is a cool way to structure your expertise that can be applied back to your **who I am** statement. It helps you frame yourself with a unique **identity**.

Start with a problem framed the following way	*Do you know how…?*	**PROBLEM**
Add how you address this problem	*Well, what I do is …*	**SOLUTION**
Explain why that's good for your 'customers'	*so that …*	**BENEFIT**
Only then do you say what you are	*I'm a …*	**SPECIALIST**
Tag on the general industry term for what you do	*Recognised role.*	

Examples might pan out like this:

Do you know how companies increase their profit by reducing the cost of the products they make? *Well, what I do is* work with them to improve their manufacturing processes, making them leaner so that they reduce the cost of production. *I'm a* lean manufacturing *consultant*.

attitude
attitude design

Do you know how people struggle to decide what career they want? *Well, what I do is* offer advice on which jobs will best fit with their personal values *so that* they find work that they enjoy more end excel at. *I'm a* career *coach.*

Do you know how companies struggle to keep up with the different technologies available to market their business? *Well, what I do is* research the technologies available and brief companies on how they work *so that* they can spend time on their marketing campaigns and not on technical stuff. *I'm a* marketing technology *analyst.*

Do you know how large companies need complex IT systems to run their businesses? *Well, what I do is* design effective ways for them to support their IT *so that* they can be confident that their business won't be interrupted by system failures. *I'm an IT* service solutions *consultant.*

The beauty of this technique is:

- It **paces** with a fact (*do you know how…*) and then **leads** (*well, what I do is…*) to what you want to influence.
- It builds **rapport** through empathy with the perspective of your 'customer'
- It **reframes** you as providing a solution to a problem in a way that expresses your value to your customer
- It wraps the **content** *(who you are)* in **context** *(who you do it for and what their problems are)* and **process** *(what you do for them)*
- It uses common industry terminology so that you don't break **rapport** but twists it with a **specialist** term that describes you in a way that gives you an **identity** as an **authority**
- It's provocative; it makes you think creatively about how you do what you do - if the way you describe yourself doesn't sound authoritative enough, it forces you to go inside and find different and interesting ways to **redefine yourself** so that you become more specialised and more of an authority.

how to be exceptional

Take permission to **make your own expert badge** – don't expect somebody else to make one for you.

Find ways to describe yourself in a way that exudes expertise with an **identity** as an **authority** figure in some **context**.

Subtly drop your experience into day-to-day conversations so that your statements and opinions become more credible.

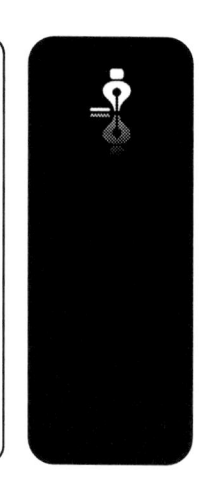

attitude
attitude design

Reputation

Your reputation is one of the most precious possessions you have as an individual. It's what you use to convince others that you are worthy of their time and attention.

Because it's so precious, you should take measures to protect it. As you would with your house or car, you should alarm your reputation to prevent it from intrusion and damage.

You can **protect your reputation** by being **consistent** in your **behaviour**.

But reputation is a strange possession because you **have** it and you **create** it. If you really want to secure your reputation, go on the offensive and create it.

In **module 4** we heard that **'you can't build a reputation on what you're going to do'**. I'd like you to reconsider this for a moment.

Your historical reputation has been built through your previous actions.

You are also constantly building your future reputation by **what you are doing now**.

> "Reputations are created every day and every minute."
>
> **Christopher Ruel**

Although I don't want you to **feel under pressure** in your day-to-day actions, you need to be very aware how your reputation is affected by everything you say and do, how you manage your **state**, how **congruent** you are, to what degree you live to your **values** and how you build, maintain and break **rapport**.

how to be exceptional

Realise that everything you do now is forming part of your reputation and that **you can create** whatever **reputation** you want **through** your **actions**.

> How would other people describe you to somebody who doesn't know you?
>
> Because, whatever you want that statement to be, you need to act in a way that influences other people to want to describe you in that way.

One key aspect of your reputation is having something that makes you stand out; you don't need to get a Mohican hairstyle or a tongue piercing but you should have a **trademark**. Something you're **reputed** for in addition to your historical reputation. Something about you that makes people recall you in a positive, or at least neutral, light.

- You know, she's the one who wears the pink shirts…
- You remember him; he's always out walking at lunch time…
- He had white football boots on…
- The one who has the really cool hair…
- She asked all those really challenging questions…
- The girl who carries that red leather folder to every meeting…
- He never stopped tackling right up to the final whistle…
- He always really thinks about what he says before he answers you…
- She's always happy and never appears stressed…
- He was the guy in the corner with the cufflinks and nice shoes…
- She always takes an interest in how you are…
- He usually wears a brown suit…

attitude
attitude design

Doing things that make you stand out in a crowd gives you a **current reputation**. Your current reputation gets you noticed so that you can discuss your **historical reputation**.

Once you've got this far, you can work on convincing people where you are going next; you can begin to create your **future reputation**.

Guard your **reputation** and constantly manage it.

Behave consistently and you will protect your reputation.

Become reputed for things that cause others to talk about you in a positive or neutral way. Don't just have a reputation, create one.

Realise that your reputation has **historical**, **current** and **future** components. Everything you do now counts towards your future reputation.

Recreation

Recreation can relate to **use of leisure time**. Or it can be associated with the process of **refreshing and revitalising** something. Let's call these **recreation** and **re-creation** respectively.

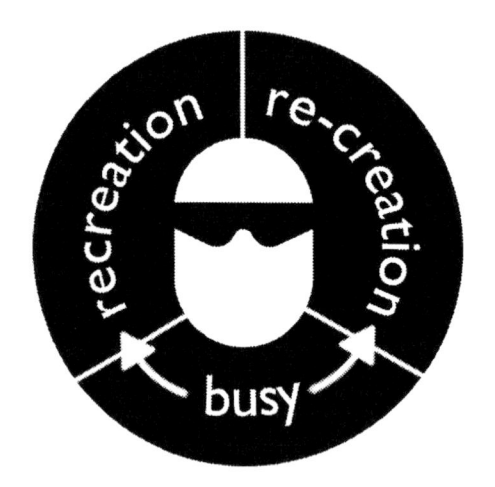

In both contexts, I believe that recreation is a crucial part of your attitude and to becoming exceptional.

Whenever you're doing something that's worthy of your time and energy, it is important that you commit and apply yourself so that you perform to your best and underpin your **reputation**.

When you finish something, you should partake in either **recreation** or **re-creation**. That's to say, you should either do something that you enjoy or you should do something that will make you even better next time.

Focused **recreation** gives you downtime; time during which you can recharge. This downtime is where you get so lost in what you're doing that you don't think about the things that you think about during the time when you're **busy** doing whatever it is you do best. Because being exceptional is a tiring business and you need time out if you're to maintain it.

Focused **re-creation** is also important. Sometimes you need to take what you've learned about yourself and incorporate it into a new you. You can gradually fold in behavioural changes that shift you from being the **usual you** to the **new you**. The new **you will be even more exceptional**.

attitude
attitude design

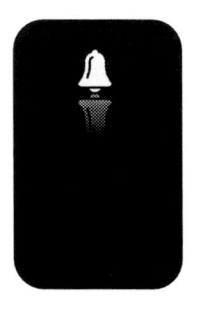

> You need to evolve. Don't assume that your genes are fixed and that the only evolution will come from the next generation.
>
> Change your genes now; periodically update the way that you do what you do so that you get better.

To re-create, you must notice. You must try things out. You need to find something to go **towards**. You must go into **bullet time**, listen to your **self talk** and notice what you **tolerate**. Try out the things that you've discovered in the modules so far. Constantly re-invent yourself based on your new awareness. Re-clarify your **values** and ensure that who you are being reflects your **dos and don'ts**.

> From this point onwards, see your time in one of three possible modes. You're either:
>
> - **busy** doing whatever you've committed to
> - **recreating**, resting and relaxing
> - **re-creating** yourself
>
> You are either doing the things you've decided to do, **or** you're creating **downtime** where your mind and body can completely re-charge **or** you're consciously **refining who you are and how you behave**.
>
> This means that from this point onwards, you have a model that enables you to ask yourself how you are using your time and whether you are dividing it between these modes enough to become exceptional.

Attitude Designer

Distinguished behavioural modeller Robert Dilts designed a method for describing how individuals behave and undergo change. His model, 'logical levels of change' offers a framework that enables you to make sense of your personality so that you better understand what you do and who you are.

Dilts' model breaks how you describe yourself into six levels.

Your **environment** – where are you when you do what you do?

Your **behaviours** – what do you do specifically when you do it?

Your **capabilities** – how do you do what you do? Which skills are you using?

Your **beliefs** – why do you do what you do? Which values drive you to do it?

Source: Robert Dilts' Logical Levels of Change

Your **identity** – who are you being when you do it?

Your **purpose** – who else are you when you do it? Or, what is your underlying reason for doing it?

When people describe what they do or define who they are, they respond at a certain level. If you think back to your **who I am** statement from module 1 and the subsequent updates you've made to it throughout the programme, you'll notice that your statements fit in with these levels.

attitude
attitude design

If you described yourself in a work context, you may have said:

statement	level	context
I work in a workshop	**Environment**	Where you work
I make furniture	**Behaviour**	What you do for a job
I shape and form wood	**Capabilities**	How you do your job
I am a cabinet maker	**Identity**	Who you're labelled as

You are less likely to have referred to your beliefs or purpose and said something like:

statement	level	context
I believe that work should involve getting paid for the things you enjoy doing the most.	**Beliefs**	Why you are driven to do this type of job
I need to help people be comfortable and enjoy their surroundings more.	**Purpose**	Some deep seated reason for being that really makes you tick

When you describe who you are on **all levels**, you find greater meaning in what you do. You don't just realise **what** you do, you also realise **who** you are when you are doing it.

There is something **above your values**; something that's there all of the time but which you rarely ask yourself. You don't ask because it's a really difficult thing to answer – even more difficult than clarifying your **values**.

> Dilts uses the word **purpose** but I think it's much more than that. Sometimes you have to go to other languages to identify words with a meaning for which we have no word. The French call it **raison d'être** - a basic, **essential purpose**; a **reason to exist**.
>
> I like to think of your **purpose** as your **primary program**; the single thing that you as an individual will revert back to for **guidance**. If you look hard enough, it's **beneath all of your actions, decisions and desires**.
>
> It's your **spiritual guide**.

It may be a single word or it may be a phrase. You can use the attitude designer to help identify it.

Starting with **environment** at the one o'clock position, write down the things that you notice about you and the things you do. You could do this with a single context in mind such as 'at work', 'when I sing' or 'at home'.

Alternatively, you could do it more generally across all of the things you do. Since your underlying **beliefs** and **purpose** are likely to be the same across which ever context you choose, the outcome is likely to be very similar however you decide to do it.

attitude
attitude design

As you consider your **environment**, think about the things around you when you do whatever it is that you do - your physical location, tools and surroundings, the people around you, the things that give you confidence, comfort, enjoyment and excitement.

Next, begin to consider what it is that you do **specifically**. What are the common traits of **behaviour** that you have – the physical and mental actions that occur as you do the things you do.

Now, focus on your skills and **capabilities**. What personal resources do you call on that enable you to do the things you do? How are you able to do these things?

Beliefs are interconnected to your **values**. You have already made a start on clarifying these so clarify them further; look for the strong values that drive the things that you do. Find the emotional magnets that pull you in a direction; the shining lights that you use as beacons or the constant humming sounds that you head towards. You'll know you've found them when you can say **'I believe that....'** and it will just make sense.

Then, consider who you are when you do the things you do; your **identity**. What is the name that you and others would give to you to describe the things that you do?

You can call on your **who I am** statement to help. Hopefully, by now, you'll have a few to choose from.

Once you have these things, ask yourself this question:

> **'What is it that deep down, makes me do what I do?'**

What's the reason that you think you exist as an individual in the context of the things that you do?

It may take some time; maybe five minutes, possibly five days. You can't rush it but you can keep asking the same fundamental questions over and over

- What's my **raison d'être**?
- What's my **primary program**?
- What's my **essential purpose**?
- What's my **reason to exist**?

When you get your first answer, go deeper; ask '**Why?**' then ask it again and again. It may come to you in the shower, in the car, on the phone or in the gym. If you ask your unconscious enough, it will respond.

> Once you find a **purpose**, you can re-consider the other five aspects of your attitude and re-design them so that they are consistent with your purpose. You become a laser guided missile – locked on to a target, tweaking every parameter available to you in the pursuit of your **primary program**.

In any order you like, ask yourself:

- How could my **environment** differ in support of this **purpose**?
- How should I **behave** in order to achieve my **purpose**?
- What **capabilities** do I have and need to reach my **purpose**?
- Which **values** and **beliefs** most underpin my **purpose**?
- Now I'm aware of my **purpose**, what should my '**who I am**' statement **REALLY** say?

attitude
attitude design

The **attitude designer** gives you a framework that you can use to **build a new attitude**. It helps you establish the **values** you hold on to and the **deeper purpose** behind your actions.

It becomes your map during **re-creation**; satellite navigation for your attitude.

Know your purpose. Find it and lock onto it. Make every aspect of your attitude consistent with it. When you do this, you'll become exceptional.

how to be exceptional

Module 9 - Exercise

You've probably already realised what you need to do next – use the Attitude Designer.

Starting with your environment, work around in a clockwise direction and list the things in each section that come to mind. Take your time and be thorough; you can go back as things come to you later.

Find your **purpose**. Once you find it write it in loud, bold, thick letters at the top of a new attitude designer circle.

Then, re-establish each level with your purpose in mind.

How would you like things to be? What identity, beliefs, capabilities, behaviours and environment would you like to create for yourself in pursuit of your purpose?

By the way, this isn't a one off exercise that you need to do in order to complete this programme. It's an exercise that you can do more regularly as you become more and more exceptional.

Happylogue

Across the nine modules, you've covered 45 models. Each model is useful in isolation and many of the models interact with each other.

You will have noticed from the first and last modules that we have completed a full cycle that you can retrace again and again. In the first module, we started with your awareness of who you were and in module nine, we completed the cycle with your map for how **you are starting to re-create yourself** and re-design your new attitude.

The models in between are tools. They give you ways of thinking about your **environment** and **behaviour**. Many of them are **capabilities** that you can use to become even more exceptional than you already are. A small number help you to focus on, clarify and update your **beliefs** and **values**. Others help you to identify, enhance and protect your **identity**.

Use them all; they work.

The key is your **purpose**. Having a strategy to re-create yourself in pursuit of your purpose is fundamental to becoming exceptional.

If you do this, you'll become an exceptional **individual**, an exceptional **performer**, exceptionally **successful** and exceptionally **happy**.

how to be exceptional

Trying on a zebra suit

In my **map of reality**, many personal development programmes and self help books suffer from a significant shortcoming – at the end, they end. This programme is different in that **the end is where it starts**.

Knowing about these models is one thing. Applying them and embedding them into your day-to-day routine is another matter.

So that you understand how to apply the models fully, I believe it's important to have them explained by people who have been involved in their development and use them successfully.

It's also useful to be able to discuss your experiences with other like-minded people.

www.zebrasuit.com is an online community created to ensure that your drive to become exceptional doesn't end here.

When you become a member of www.zebrasuit.com, you gain access to a live training programme and constantly evolving material relating to the 45 models covered in this programme.

Live training takes the form of short tele-classes that you dial in to using a UK local rate telephone number. In each session, an experienced trainer covers one or more models in detail to strengthen your understanding.

As a member, you can also contribute your own experience of the models and read the comments and experiences of other members. This turns the theory into practise and allows you to benefit from the knowledge of a whole community of exceptional people.

The material on www.zebrasuit.com is indexed using the 45 models so that you can quickly find material relevant to the important aspects of your development.

New and interesting material is added continually so that you benefit from a dynamic training environment that accelerates your **drive to be exceptional**.

www.zebrasuit.com

Guide to using the models

The 45 models covered in this programme are ways of thinking. I couldn't imagine using all of them in the same week let alone being flexible enough to use them all at the same time.

I frequently use a certain response when I work on consulting assignments. When I'm asked for advice or for an answer to a problem, I often respond by saying **'it depends'**. I use it frequently because it's so often true.

How you decide to do something depends on what outcome you're trying to achieve and it's exactly the same with these models.

If you've followed the exercises on the programme and completed the attitude designer, you'll have a good understanding whether you need to work on your **environment, behaviours, capabilities, beliefs, identity** or **purpose**.

On your journey through the models, you will have realised which ones can be of benefit to you straight away and which are on the edge of your comfort zone and may require some practise.

The table over the page summarises the models in the context of the different levels of the **attitude designer** so that you can plot a development path.

You could choose to focus on one of the main modules such as, **impact** or **attraction**. Alternatively, you could choose to focus on one of the attitude designer levels such as your **identity** or **behaviour**.

Just make sure you do something. If you want to be exceptional, hope isn't really a strategy.

how to be exceptional

		Environment	Behaviour	Capabilities	Beliefs	Identity	Purpose	
Know yourself	States		◉					Awareness
	TEA			◉				
	Maps of reality			◉				
	Values				◉			
	Who I am					◉		
Impact	Gravitas bow tie					◉		Presence
	Contextual healing			◉				
	Transmit vs. Receive		◉					
	Intensity x Frequency			◉				
	Outcomes & Styles					◉		
Positive Mind	Facts vs. Attitudes			◉				Attitude
	Self Talk			◉				
	Tolerations			◉				
	Reframing			◉				
	Anchoring	◉						
	Beware Infection	◉						
Strengths First	Tribal archetypes					◉		Awareness
	Journey to today					◉		
	Welcome your weaknesses			◉				
	Failure vs. Feedback			◉				
	Dos & Don'ts				◉			
Influence	Rapport		◉					Presence
	Being vague			◉				
	Principles vs. Specifics			◉				
	Unconscious Influence			◉				
	Hot / Cold & Push / Pull			◉				

		Environment	Behaviour	Capabilities	Beliefs	Identity	Purpose	
Behaviour Tuning	Bullet Time		⊙					**Attitude**
	Congruence		⊙					
	Head vs. Heart		⊙					
	Away vs. Towards		⊙					
	Intuiting to Action			⊙				
Awareness of others	Motives				⊙			**Awareness**
	People are their emotions			⊙				
	Pictures, Sounds & Feelings			⊙				
	Filters on reality	⊙						
	Perception			⊙				
Attraction	How are you today?					⊙		**Presence**
	Being interesting					⊙		
	Totems & Cults				⊙			
	Submodalities			⊙				
	Rich language			⊙				
Attitude design	Be an expert or authority					⊙		**Attitude**
	Reputation					⊙		
	Recreation						⊙	
	Attitude Designer						⊙	

how to be exceptional

Recommended reading

Certain books and websites make you think differently. The following have been a great source of inspiration and intervention for me.

book	author
Serious Creativity: Using the Power of Lateral Thinking to Create New Ideas	Edward de Bono
The Four-fold Way: Walking the Paths of the Warrior, Teacher, Healer and Visionary	Angeles Arrien
The 48 Laws of power	Robert Greene, Joost Ellfers
An insider's guide to submodalities	Richard Bandler, Will Macdonald
Built to last	James C. Collins, Jerry I. Porras
Now discover your strengths	Marcus Buckingham
Monsters and Magical Sticks: Or, There's No Such Thing As Hypnosis	Steven Heller, Terry Lee Steele
The Structure of Magic Vol. I & II	John Grinder, Richard Bandler
Tranceformations	Richard Bandler

websites

Discovering what you're really good at	www.kolbe.com
Finding random things and interesting facts	www.stumbleupon.com
Satisfying your hunger for knowledge	www.wikipedia.org
Expanding your range of rich language	www.visualthesaurus.com
Finding inspirational quotations	www.quotationspage.com
Finding inspirational imagery	www.istockphoto.com
	www.morguefile.com